AMERICA ONLINE

Gene Steinberg

in 10 Minutes

SAMS

A Division of Macmillan Computer Publishing
201 West 103rd St., Indianapolis, Indiana, 46290 USA

EXECUTIVE EDITOR
Angie Wethington

ACQUISITIONS EDITOR
Stephanie McComb

DEVELOPMENT EDITOR
John Gosney

TECHNICAL EDITOR
Mark Hall

MANAGING EDITOR
Thomas F. Hayes

PROJECT EDITOR
Lori A. Lyons

COPY EDITORS
Kate Givens
Pat Kinyon

INDEXER
Joy Dean Lee

PRODUCTION
Brad Lenser
Carl Pierce

OVERVIEW

Introduction

1 GETTING AND INSTALLING AOL SOFTWARE

2 SETTING UP YOUR AOL SOFTWARE

3 GETTING ACQUAINTED WITH AOL

4 DOING BUSINESS ON AOL

5 SHOPPING ON AOL

6 GETTING ENTERTAINED ON AOL

7 GETTING INFORMED ON AOL

8 USING AOL EMAIL

9 USING INSTANT MESSAGES AND INSTANT MESSENGER

10 USING AOL MESSAGE BOARDS

11 JOINING AND PARTICIPATING IN AN AOL CHAT

12 VISITING THE INTERNET ON AOL

13 MAKING WEB PAGES IN AN INSTANT

14 USING OTHER INTERNET SOFTWARE WITH AOL

15 SETTING UP AUTOMATIC AOL SESSIONS

16 FINDING AND DOWNLOADING SOFTWARE FROM AOL

17   USING AOL'S MEMBER HELP FORUMS

18   COMMON SOLUTIONS TO COMMON PROBLEMS

19   AOL'S NEIGHBORHOOD WATCH

INDEX

CONTENTS

Introduction xiii

1   GETTING AND INSTALLING AOL SOFTWARE   1

Getting and Installing the Software 1
Installing AOL's Software..2
New to Windows 95 or Windows 98? 3
Installing AOL's Windows 95/98 Software 3
Installing AOL's Windows 3.X Software 4
Choosing an Installation Option..4
Adding AOL to Your Windows 95 Start Menu...................................5
Setting Up AOL's Software...6
Finding a Local Connection 8
Joining AOL 9
Establishing Your AOL Address 10
AOL's Terms of Service 12
Welcome to AOL 12

2   SETTING UP YOUR AOL SOFTWARE   14

Finding New Access Numbers 14
Finding Numbers When You're Signed On 17
Configuring AOL's Software 18
Using an AOL Keyword 19
AOL's Keyboard Shortcuts 20
Using AOL's Toolbar 22

3   GETTING ACQUAINTED WITH AOL   26

Visiting AOL Channels..26
Where *Is* It? Using AOL's Find Central 28
Visiting an AOL Forum 33
AOL's Online Conferences 34
AOL Keywords You Need 34

4   DOING BUSINESS ON AOL   36

Using AOL's WorkPlace Channel..36
Using PrimeHost, AOL's Web Hosting Service 37

Using AOL's Personal Finance Channel..39
Using AOL's Quotes and Portfolios Feature 41
AOL's Tax Forums 42

5   SHOPPING ON AOL   45

Visiting AOL's Shopping Channel 45
Ordering Merchandise from AOL...46
Advertising on AOL 48
Before You Shop Online 49
Visiting AOL's Travel Channel 50

6   GETTING ENTERTAINED ON AOL   53

Visiting the Entertainment Channel 53
AOL's Movies Forums 54
Visiting AOL's Games Channel 55
Exploring AOL's Sports Channel 57

7   GETTING INFORMED ON AOL   60

Using AOL's News Channel 60
Receive Top News Stories Automatically...62
Read Magazines and Newspapers Online 63
Exploring the Influence Channel 63
A Brief Look at AOL's Research & Learn Channel..........................64
Using AOL's Ask-A-Teacher Service 66

8   USING AOL EMAIL   68

How to Use Electronic Mail on AOL 68
Sending Email with Style 69
Sending AOL Email 70
Email Is Not Just for Text...71
Sending Internet Email 71
Receiving Email 72
Answering Email 74
Sending Email with Attached Files 75
How to Save Email 76
Using AOL's Address Book 77

9   USING INSTANT MESSAGES AND INSTANT MESSENGER   79

Using AOL Instant Messages 79
Using Instant Messenger for Internet Communications 82
Using the Buddy List 83
Finding AOL Members 86

10   USING AOL MESSAGE BOARDS   88

How Do Message Boards Differ from Email? 88
How Message Boards are Organized 89
Checking Message Board Postings....................................90
Using Message Board Preferences 92
Visiting Message Boards for the First Time......................93
Message Board Ground Rules 95
How to Post a Message..96
Reviewing Online Etiquette 97
Where's the Response? 98

11   JOINING AND PARTICIPATING IN AN AOL CHAT   99

Using AOL's Online Chat Feature 99
What's a Chat and What's a Conference? 99
Entering a Chat Room 99
Attending Online Conferences 101
How to Participate in an Online Conference 102
How to Behave in a Chat Room 104
A Brief Description of Chat Protocol...............................104
Online Shorthand 104

12   VISITING THE INTERNET ON AOL   106

Using AOL's Internet Features 106
AOL's Internet Services 106
Using AOL's Web Browser..108
Using AOL's Newsgroup Feature 109
Transferring Files on the Internet 110
Finding Information on the Internet 111
Using AOL's Mailing List Feature 112
Using AOL's Bring Your Own Access Plan 113
AOL and Internet Providers—What's the Difference?......113
How to Connect to AOL via an ISP 113

13   MAKING WEB PAGES IN AN INSTANT   115

Before You Start 115
Using AOL's Personal Publisher....................................116
Choosing a Template 117
Writing a Title and Headline 118
Adding Background Artwork 118
Adding Pictures to Your Page...119
Adding Text 120
Done Yet? 121
Where's That Page? 122
Web Service for Businesses 123

**14   USING OTHER INTERNET SOFTWARE
       WITH AOL   124**

You're Not Stuck with AOL's Own Web Browser 124
The Limits of Using Other Net Software.........................126
Using Internet Chat Software 127
First the Software 127
Setting Up an IRC Client Program..................................128
Using Your New IRC Software...129
The Next Step... 130
Finding Other Internet Chats 132

15   SETTING UP AUTOMATIC AOL SESSIONS   133

Using Automatic AOL 133
Automatic Email...134
Automatic File Transfers 136
Automatic Message Board Visits 136
Password Settings 136
Scheduling the Sessions 137
Where's the Email Stored?...139

**16   FINDING AND DOWNLOADING SOFTWARE
       FROM AOL   140**

AOL's Software Libraries Often Come First 140
Using Virus Protection Software 140
Finding the Files You Want..141
How to Download Files 143
Using the Download Later Option 144

How to Use the Files You've Downloaded 146
Resuming File Downloads 146
Finding the File 147
What Kind of Software is There on AOL? 147

17   USING AOL'S MEMBER HELP FORUMS   149

Using the Member Help Forums 149
Visiting the Member Service Area 149
AOL's Download Help Center 150
Getting Help from Other Members 151
Getting Interactive Support from AOL 152

18   COMMON SOLUTIONS TO COMMON PROBLEMS   155

Getting Over the Rough Spots 155
Old Version Still Installed? 155
Mess Up Your Toolbar? 155
Do You Use a Macintosh Too? 156
Solutions to Common Modem Problems 156
Is AOL Off the Air? 159
Where's My Sound? 159
Why's the Request Taking So Long? 159
Why Do They Want My Password? 160
My Message Board Post Disappeared 160
Unsolicited Email 160
Where Did That Web Site Go? 161
Why's My Web Performance So Slow? 161
Can't Connect via FTP? 162
System Crashing? 162

19   AOL'S NEIGHBORHOOD WATCH   163

AOL Is Usually Friendly, but... 163
Visiting Neighborhood Watch 164
Using Parental Controls 165
Setting Custom Parental Controls 166
Setting Mail Controls 167
AOL's Terms of Service 168
Reporting Problems 168

INDEX   171

ACKNOWLEDGMENTS

I'd like to thank the team at Sams for making this book a pleasure to write and ensuring that every word was checked and double-checked for accuracy. I'm also grateful to the kind assistance of Lew Grimes for his sage advice, and to AOL's corporate communications staff for providing the information I needed to describe the latest versions of AOL's software.

And a heartfelt thanks to my wife, Barbara, and my son, Grayson, for putting up with the long hours I spent chained to my computer so that the book could be finished on schedule.

TRADEMARKS

All terms mentioned in this book that are known to be trademarks or service marks have been appropriately capitalized. Sams Publishing cannot attest to the accuracy of this information. Use of a term in this book should not be regarded as affecting the validity of any trademark or service mark.

ABOUT THE AUTHOR

Gene Steinberg is an inveterate desktop computer user who first joined America Online in 1989. He quickly became addicted to the online service and finally earned positions in its Computing channel. He currently runs the AOL Portrait Gallery (which features photos of members and their families).

In his regular life, Gene has worked at several occupations. He first studied broadcasting and then worked for a number of years as a disc jockey and newscaster. Gene is now a full-time writer (fact and science fiction) and computer software and systems consultant. His latest published work includes *Using America Online 4.0* for Que Corporation.

TELL US WHAT YOU THINK

As a reader, you are the most important critic and commentator of our books. We value your opinion and want to know what we're doing right, what we could do better, what areas you'd like to see us publish in, and any other words of wisdom you're willing to pass our way. You can help us make strong books that meet your needs and give you the computer guidance you require.

If you have access to the World Wide Web, check out our site at http://www.mcp.com. If you have a technical question about this book, call the technical support line at (317)581-3833 or send email to support@mcp.com.

Your comments will help us to continue publishing the best books available on computer topics in today's market. You can contact us at

Publisher
Sams Publishing
201 West 103rd Street
Indianapolis, IN 46290
USA

INTRODUCTION

AOL is the number-one online service in the world. They didn't get that way overnight. It all started out very humbly in the mid-1980s, as AOL was founded as a service for users of the Commodore computer.

Of course, the Commodore is no more, but AOL changed with the times. They expanded the service to Apple Macintosh computers and to Microsoft Windows, and as the years progressed, they added the latest Internet and multimedia services, to provide the most features and a consistent, easy-to-use interface.

AOL is huge—a sprawling supermarket of forums, message areas, chat rooms—and ever-present is fast access to the Internet. Although it's designed for both novice and experienced computer users, it's really easy to get lost in the maze of so many features.

Sams Teach Yourself America Online in 10 Minutes is designed for people just like you. In these pages, you learn how to join AOL and then how to get the most value from the service. And it's all presented as a series of short, easy-to-understand lessons. Each lesson is self-contained and can be completed in 10 minutes or less, so you can start and stop as your schedule allows. There's no padding in this book, and no unnecessary or highly technical details. It's loaded with clear, concise information that you can really use.

WHAT IS TEACH YOURSELF AOL IN 10 MINUTES?

This series takes a different approach to teaching people how to use a computer program. We do not attempt to cover every detail of the program. Instead, each book concentrates on the program features that are essential for most users, the features that you need to get your work done. Our goal is to teach you, as quickly and painlessly as possible, those things you need to start using the AOL and get the most value from it.

USING THIS BOOK

Sams Teach Yourself America Online in 10 Minutes contains a total of 19 lessons. Ideally, you should work through them in order. The first three lessons show you how to join AOL, configure the software to your liking, and then take you for a breezy tour around the service. After reading these lessons, however, you can skip around to find specific information as quickly as possible. When you complete the book, you should have a good knowledge of the most important parts of AOL, which will greatly enhance your enjoyment of the service and the ease with which you access the content areas you want.

Several special elements are used throughout the book to highlight specific types of information.

 Tip These tips offer shortcuts and hints for using AOL most effectively.

 Plain English These identify new terms and definitions.

 Caution These appear in places where new users often run into trouble.

Several other of the book's features are designed to make your learning faster and easier:

- Numbered steps provide exact instructions for commonly needed procedures.

- Menu commands, toolbar buttons, and dialog box options that you select are printed in blue for easy recognition.

- Text that you enter is **boldface and blue.**

- Messages that appear onscreen are **boldface.**

LESSON 1

GETTING AND INSTALLING AOL SOFTWARE

In this lesson, you learn how to order and install AOL's software.

GETTING AND INSTALLING THE SOFTWARE

It's easy to obtain a copy of AOL software—in fact, you probably already have it. It's usually bundled with your new computer in the Online Services directory on your Windows desktop, and it's packaged with many magazines and books.

If you don't have a copy on hand, call AOL at 1-800-827-6364 and they'll send you a copy. In the meantime, you'll probably want to review the basic steps for getting online and checking out the service before the software arrives.

 Is Your PC Compatible with AOL? Before ordering AOL software, you should make sure that your PC will be able to use the new software. You can find a listing of minimum system needs in the following section, "Installing AOL's Software." AOL's software comes in separate versions for users of Windows 3.1, Windows 95 or 98, or the Mac OS.

INSTALLING AOL's SOFTWARE

When you have an AOL software disk or CD on hand, you'll want to double-check that you have a computer capable of running it. For AOL 4, the version covered in this book, you need either of the following:

- **Windows 3.1**:

    486-based or better PC

    12MB (megabytes) RAM

    30MB available hard disk space

    A monitor capable of displaying at least 640×480 with 256 colors or better

    A 14,400bps (bits per second) or faster modem (28,800bps recommended)

- **Windows 95**:

    Pentium-based PC

    16MB RAM

    30MB available hard disk space

    A monitor capable of displaying at least 640×480 with 256 colors or better

    A 14,400bps or faster modem (28,800bps recommended)

 Faster Modems Are Even Better! Although AOL recommends a 28,800bps modem for good performance, the new generation of 56K modems are even better. They offer a more delightful online experience because screen displays (especially from Web sites) appear faster on your PC. AOL has been in the forefront of adding high-speed technology to their service. And the latest high-speed modems don't cost much more than the lower speed models.

NEW TO WINDOWS 95 OR WINDOWS 98?

This book is written with the assumption that you know the basics of using Windows 95 or Windows 98, such as navigating through directories, accessing menu bar commands, using the mouse, and so on.

 Get Ready to Join AOL! Before you install AOL, you'll want to have your billing information handy (so AOL knows how you want to pay for the account). You'll also want to make sure your modem is turned on. And don't forget that little slip of paper that comes with AOL's software, which has the registration number and password you need to set up your account.

INSTALLING AOL'S WINDOWS 95/98 SOFTWARE

AOL's clever software installer guides you through the necessary steps. All you have to do is read the prompts as you go along and make the proper selections

1. Insert the AOL CD-ROM into your PC's CD drive (or the disk into your PC's drive—A or B).

2. Using the Start menu, choose Settings, Control Panel, and then double-click the Add/Remove Programs utility.

3. On the first screen of the Add/Remove Programs Properties screen, click the Install button.

4. When the AOL program installer is located, click the Finish button to begin the installation process as shown in Figure 1.1 (yes, I know it seems like a contradiction).

Choose your installation option before you begin.

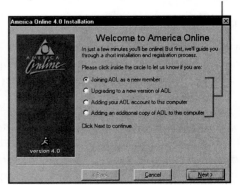

FIGURE 1.1 Follow the information prompts as the software installation progresses.

INSTALLING AOL'S WINDOWS 3.X SOFTWARE

To install the Windows 3.x version of AOL's software, follow these steps:

1. Insert the America Online CD-ROM into your PC's CD drive (or the disk into your PC's drive—A or B).

2. In the Program Manager, go to the File menu and select the Run command.

3. Depending on which drive you inserted the disk in, type either **a:\setup** or **b:\setup** (or indicate the drive that has your installation CD). Then press Enter.

CHOOSING AN INSTALLATION OPTION

To proceed with the installation, you'll need to tell the software installer whether you have an existing AOL version on your computer's drive to update, or whether you want to do a fresh, clean install of the new version. I'm going to assume you're signing up as a new member when you read this section, so check the first option—this one puts in a full copy of AOL's software without touching any other version you might have.

The progress of the installation is shown onscreen (see Figure 1.2).

If you need to stop the installation, click here.

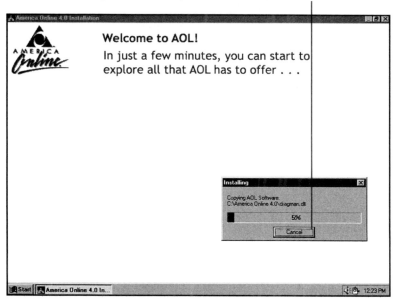

FIGURE 1.2 The status of your AOL software setup is indicated by a progress bar.

 Keep Your Windows 95 or Windows 98 Setup Disk Handy! The AOL software installer sometimes needs files from your Windows 95 or Windows 98 Setup disks, so to avoid any delays in setting up the software, you'll want to have these disks (or CD) ready. You'll see an onscreen message requesting the disk if files are needed from it.

ADDING AOL TO YOUR WINDOWS 95 START MENU

At the very end of the AOL software setup process, you'll see a dialog box asking whether you want to put your AOL software on the Start menu. This is an option you'll probably want to OK.

Don't Skip the ReadMe! Just before the AOL's software installation is done, you'll see a ReadMe on your PC's screen. You'll want to scroll through it, or print it for later review. This ReadMe covers the basics of AOL's software features, and lists some online areas you'll want to check out after you join.

After the software installation is complete, you see one of two options:

- *Restart Windows.* This is an option you need to OK to make sure AOL's software runs properly.

- *Whether to start AOL then and there.* If a restart isn't necessary, you still have the option to start the software and join the service.

SETTING UP AOL'S SOFTWARE

If you have to restart Windows, you see an AOL icon in your Windows 95 taskbar when you return to your Windows 95 desktop. To start the program, double-click the AOL icon. From there, you are taken through the following procedures:

1. As soon as the program opens, you're guided step-by-step through the setup process. Before making a selection, read the instructions carefully. As America Online software is updated, the information is likely to change.

2. Choose the Begin Automatic Setup option on the screen (see Figure 1.3). AOL's software checks your modem for the information it needs to work best with it.

 Do You Already Have a Net Connection? If you are already hooked up to the Internet through an Internet service provider (ISP), AOL gives you the option to use that connection to access AOL. If you choose to use your existing Internet connection rather than AOL's own network, you'll also be eligible for a lower monthly price for AOL's service.

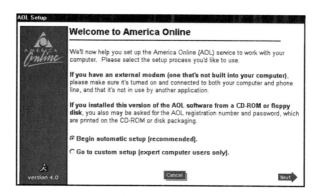

FIGURE 1.3 When you check the Automatic Setup option, AOL goes to work to find out what kind of connection you have.

3. After an intermediate screen shows you that AOL is checking your modem connection, you'll see a similar result, shown in Figure 1.4.

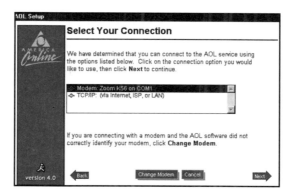

FIGURE 1.4 AOL's software tries to guess what kind of modem you have.

Did AOL's Setup Process Make a Mistake? If AOL's software selected the wrong make and model of the modem you have, click the Change Modem button (on the screen shown in Figure 1.4) and follow the information screens to select a more suitable model.

Usually, most models from a particular manufacturer use the same basic setup, so if the model isn't quite right, it might not matter.

FINDING A LOCAL CONNECTION

Hang in there—we're almost done. Now AOL's host computer has to find a local connection number for you (see Figure 1.5). As soon as your modem setup is complete, you are asked to enter your area code so America Online can hook you up to the closest, fastest (and thus cheapest) access point in your area.

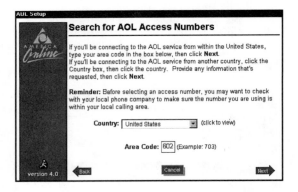

FIGURE 1.5 Choose your Area Code in this handy dialog box, and then click Next.

When you select an area code, AOL's host computer is dialed up and the current list of connection numbers is checked. If AOL cannot locate a number that's in that area code, you have the option to choose another number from a nearby area code. But there usually will be one or more numbers available for you to try (see Figure 1.6).

You'll want to pick at least two connection numbers if they are available. That way, if your modem cannot make a connection with the first number—perhaps because it's busy or because of line noise—you have another chance to connect to America Online. Each number you add produces a confirmation screen. You need to OK that screen to go to the next step in the sign-up process.

Click to choose the selected number.

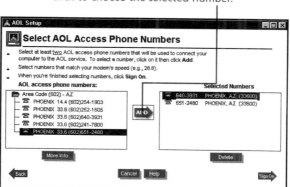

FIGURE **1.6** You choose your AOL connection numbers from this screen.

JOINING AOL

AOL now takes you through several setup screens that are needed to set up your account information and your screen name. You'll want to read each one carefully to set up your account properly. Here are the basic steps:

1. Locate the registration numbers on your America Online software package. Enter the certificate number and certificate passwords in the blank Certificate Number and Certificate Password text boxes. You can use the Tab key to move from one entry text box to the next.

2. Click Continue.

3. Enter your name, mailing address, and telephone number.

4. Click Continue.

5. Tell AOL how you want to pay for the service. You can bill your online charges via American Express, Discover Card, MasterCard, or Visa. If you prefer, you can have your monthly online charges deducted from your checking account (an extra monthly charge is applied for this option).

It Takes Longer to Bill via Checking Account If you want to pay for your AOL bill by a checking account draft, it might take several days for AOL to verify your account. During that time you won't be able to log on, so be patient.

All your account information is checked by AOL before your account is set up. If the program encounters a problem setting up your account, the account setup process will stop until you are able to update your billing information. This is done for your protection, not to make it harder to join.

ESTABLISHING YOUR AOL ADDRESS

When you join an online service, you identify yourself by an email or log-in address (which is a unique way the service uses to identify you).

The next step in your AOL sign-up process is to pick the name you'll use on the service. AOL calls it a *screen name,* which is how I'll refer to it from now on. Your screen name can include from 3 to 10 characters (letters and numbers). I should mention that 16-character names were being considered when this book was written, so this situation might change.

The easiest thing to do is try to use your real name as your AOL screen name, but if you have a common name, such as Bob or Gene, you might find that other members have taken it. AOL lets you know if the name has been taken, and suggests an alternate, which is based on the name you used in setting up your account.

This is your chance to show originality. You don't have to pick something resembling your real name. You can choose a name that reflects a personality trait, or the special look you want to present to the public. One of my online friends used to call himself simply *Bear,* and I'll let you imagine what that signified.

Only One Name at a Time! You can create up to four additional screen names on your account aside from your original account name, but you can only use one of them at a time, even if you have more than one computer, modem, and so on. If you want to use more than one name at a time, you must set up more than one account (each is billed separately).

Your Initial Login Name Can't Be Changed! You cannot change or delete your master account name without deleting your account, so take as much time as you need to select an appropriate screen name. You might also want to be careful about choosing a name that someone isn't going to use to poke fun at you (even though a silly name might seem all right when you are meeting a close friend or relative).

After America Online has accepted your screen name, your next step is to select a password. A password is your ounce of protection against someone using your account without your permission, so don't use anything obvious, such as a contraction of your name. Select a unique word that someone wouldn't stumble on at random. A mix of numbers and letters, or even punctuation marks, is a good option. For additional security, you might want to change your password from time to time.

Don't Lose Your Password! When you pick a screen name and password, write it down and place that information in a safe place. That way, if you forget your password, you can find it again quickly when you need it. If you do lose your password, you can call AOL's customer service line and they will reset it for you (after you verify your identity), so you can select another. And remember, don't give out your password! *AOL will never ask you for your password or credit card information,* so ignore any requests you receive while online for that information!

AOL's TERMS OF SERVICE

After you've set up your AOL account, you'll be asked to accept the Terms of Service (TOS). The Terms of Service are the rules and regulations that apply to AOL. Carefully read the information displayed. You also can check the text of AOL's Member Services area, but basically it requests that you be a good citizen during your online visits and avoid using vulgar language.

The Screen Name and Real Name Aren't Always the Same! Please don't forget that all AOL members are known online by their screen names, rather than their real names (which might or might not be totally different). If you decide to write an email message to another member, contact them by their screen name; otherwise, you might end up writing to the wrong person.

Log-on The act of connecting to your online service.

WELCOME TO AOL

When you first sign on to AOL, you'll see:

- *Welcome.* You hear the announcement on your PC's speaker, and see the Welcome window (see Figure 1.7).

Why Does That Screen Look Different? AOL updates its service artwork very often—sometimes several times a day. The illustrations you see in this book might have changed by the time you actually join AOL. But the actual steps you take to join and use AOL will remain pretty much the same.

Click to visit AOL's
online departments.

Click to read your email.

Click any of these
items to see more.

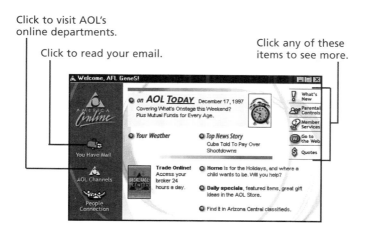

FIGURE 1.7 You've already got mail when you first log on to AOL.

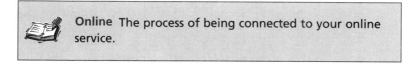

Online The process of being connected to your online
service.

- *You Have Mail.* Click this icon to read your first AOL email, a
  welcome message from the service's outspoken chief executive,
  Steve Casez.

- *Goodbye.* To end your session, choose Sign Off from the Sign
  Off menu.

If you want to close your AOL program, choose Exit from the File menu
(which logs you off first if you're still online).

In this lesson, you installed AOL's software and set up your new account.
In the next lesson, I'll show you how to customize the software for new
setup numbers and for best performance.

LESSON 2

SETTING UP YOUR AOL SOFTWARE

In this lesson, you will learn how to locate additional access numbers for AOL and configure the software the way you like.

FINDING NEW ACCESS NUMBERS

When you set up AOL's software for the first time, you choose the phone numbers needed to connect to the service. If you travel a lot, plan to move, or want to try another number to see if it works better, you'll find that getting additional access numbers is pretty simple.

 Why Use Another Number? AOL is growing so fast, some access numbers aren't set up to handle the demand. So you might try one phone number and get constant busy signals or poor performance (slow downloads of Web sites, and so on). If this is the case, see if there's another phone number in your locality and try that instead and see if it works better.

If you haven't already done so, launch the America Online program. It's a good idea to make a new Location setting for each city or area code for which you're choosing numbers. Follow these steps next:

1. Open your AOL software and click the Setup button.

2. Click the Add Location button, which opens the screen shown in Figure 2.1.

Type the number of times you want to redial the number if it's busy.

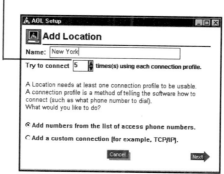

FIGURE 2.1 You can make a new location setting from this screen.

3. Give your Location setting a name. You probably want to enter the city for which the numbers apply, as I did in Figure 2.1.

4. Click the Next button (see Figure 2.2) to check AOL's database for access numbers.

Choose a country other than the USA if you're searching for foreign access numbers.

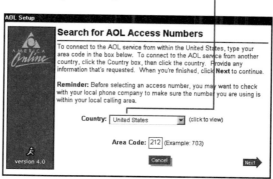

FIGURE 2.2 Enter the area code in AOL's Search for AOL Access Numbers window.

5. Type in the area code or country for which you want a number. (You might have to call the phone company if you don't know the area code.) Then click the Next button to open the list of available numbers (see Figure 2.3).

What If AOL Can't Find the Numbers? AOL stores a database of its available phone numbers on your computer's drive. If the file becomes unreadable or needs to be updated, AOL has to dial in to its access center (a toll-free number in the USA) to locate the latest listing, which might take a few minutes to complete. If AOL cannot locate a number for the area you select, you are given the chance to choose another area code or country.

Choose the number from this list.

This column indicates the maximum connection speed available if you pick this access number.

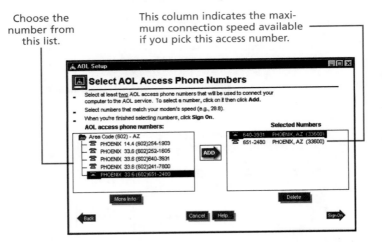

FIGURE 2.3 The list of available AOL access numbers is shown on the left side of the screen.

6. Click a number on the left once to select it, and then click the Add button, which places the number on the right side of the screen.

7. Repeat this process for each phone number that you want to select. For each number you add, there is an acknowledgment screen. Click OK to continue.

8. To remove a number, select it from the list on the right and click Remove.

Change the Dialing Order! After numbers have been added to the list, you can change the order in which they're dialed (in case one number works better than another). Just click a number from the list at the right side of the screen (the cursor changes to a grabber hand), and drag it up or down. AOL always dials numbers in the order listed, top to bottom.

9. Click Done to finish up and store your new access numbers in your copy of AOL's software.

 It's Easy to Switch Locations You can switch the Location to which your selected numbers apply by clicking the drop-down menu under the item labeled **Selected Numbers will be Added to the Location Shown.**

FINDING NUMBERS WHEN YOU'RE SIGNED ON

If you're already signed on to AOL, you can locate additional access locations by choosing AOL Access Phone Numbers from the Help menu. You can then follow the exact steps described above to set up new locations and connection numbers.

 Not All AOL Access Numbers Are Free! You pay extra if you use AOL's 800 and 888 phone numbers, some AOL numbers in Canada, and AOL's GlobalNet service in other parts of the world. Check the updated rates shown in the Access area before using any of these numbers so that you won't see any unexpected surprises added to your AOL bill. At the time this book was written, 800 and 888 access resulted in a surcharge of $6.00 per hour (or 10 cents per minute or fraction thereof).

CONFIGURING AOL'S SOFTWARE

To set up AOL's software, choose My AOL from the My AOL toolbar's drop-down menu. This produces the My AOL screen shown in Figure 2.4.

Personal Features settings

People settings for keeping in touch with your online friends

Take charge of your child's online experience.

Preferences Guide for AOL program settings

Read your email.

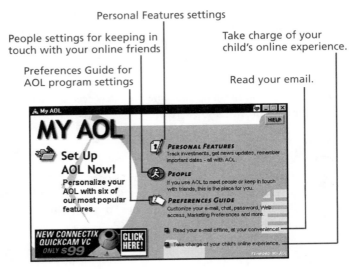

FIGURE 2.4 Use this screen to make your AOL settings.

You have five sets of preferences to set. Each setting is accessed by clicking on the labeled icon:

- *Personal Features.* Set up AOL to send you reminders of important events, check your investment portfolio, and receive the latest news on the subjects you select in your online mailbox.

- *People.* AOL is the ideal place to meet others by using chat rooms, email, and message boards. This set of preferences (see Figure 2.5) lets you create a Buddy List that shows you when your friends are online, an Address Book of your regular contacts, a member profile, and an AOL Member Directory. I cover more of these features in Lesson 9, "Using Instant Messages and Instant Messenger."

FIGURE 2.5 Keep track of your online friends and put yourself in the Member Directory with this setup feature.

- *Preferences Guide.* AOL lets you set up program preferences in 14 categories. These preferences let you decide such things as how your email is displayed, whether to store your online password, and which font is used to display AOL text.

- *Offline Reading.* You have the option to read and post messages and email offline, and then run an automated online session to do your bidding. The feature, called Automatic AOL, is set up in just a few seconds, and lets you set the time for your AOL sessions. And if you leave your computer on, you don't even have to be present when the session runs. I cover this feature in more detail in Lesson 14, "Using Other Internet Software with AOL."

- *Parental Controls.* AOL has a feature that lets you customize the online environment for your kids to provide the safest possible online experience. The ability to work with families is one of the factors that made AOL the world's number one online service. This feature is covered in Lesson 19, "AOL's Neighborhood Watch."

USING AN AOL KEYWORD

One of the best AOL shortcuts is the *keyword.* This is a keyboard command that you can use *only* while you're connected to America Online.

A keyword can take you just about anywhere on America Online, even if you don't know the exact route.

To use keywords, press Ctrl+K, and then enter the keyword in the entry text box of the Keyword dialog box displayed on your screen (see Figure 2.6). Now press the Return or Enter key and, in just a few seconds, you go right to the place you want to visit. (Of course, if the keyword is wrong, you get a message to that effect; you can then click the Search button to view some suggestions that might match your quest.)

Click to reach the online area.

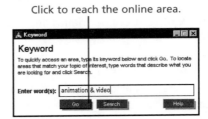

FIGURE 2.6 Use keywords to get around AOL quickly.

 Another Way to Use an AOL Keyword You also can call up a keyword by entering the place you want to visit in the text box on the bottom row of your AOL program toolbar and clicking the Go button. You get there just as quickly.

 Want to Check Your Bill? You can examine your AOL statement at any time via the keyword **Billing**. You can also use that area to change your billing plan (perhaps you want to use a different credit card) or sign up for another pricing plan.

AOL's KEYBOARD SHORTCUTS

Table 2.1 lists many keyboard shortcuts available with your America Online Windows software. They are based on the version of AOL software available at the time this book was written. You'll find additional options if you use the right mouse button when accessing AOL's features.

 Use Favorite Places for Fast Access! When you see a little heart-shaped icon at the right of an AOL area's title bar, it means you can add it to your Favorite Places list. Just click the icon, choose the first option in the next screen to add it to your Favorite Places list, and you're finished. To access the list, choose the Favorites icon's drop-down menu.

TABLE 2.1 **AOL KEYBOARD SHORTCUTS**

FUNCTION	KEYBOARD SHORTCUT
Cancel an action	Esc
Cascade windows	Shift+F5
Check spelling	Ctrl+=
Close a window	Ctrl+F4
Compose mail	Ctrl+M
Copy	Ctrl+C
Cut	Ctrl+X
Find in Top Window	Ctrl+F
Get member profile	Ctrl+G
Keyword (go to)	Ctrl+K
Locate a member online	Ctrl+L
Move to next button	Tab
Move to next window	Ctrl+F6
Move to previous button	Shift+Tab
My Shortcuts menu	Ctrl+1 through Ctrl+0

continues

Table 2.1   CONTINUED

FUNCTION	KEYBOARD SHORTCUT
Open a new text file	Ctrl+N
Open an existing file	Ctrl+O
Open Keyword window	Ctrl+K
Open Mail window	Ctrl+M
Paste	Ctrl+V
Print Document	Ctrl+P
Read mail	Ctrl+R
Save a file	Ctrl+S
Scroll down a page	Page Down
Scroll up a page	Page Up
Send an instant message	Ctrl+I
Send instant message or email	Ctrl+Enter
Tile windows	Shift+F4
Undo action	Ctrl+Z

 AOL Remembers Where You've Been Click the arrow icon at the right of the text field on the bottom row of the toolbar. You see a drop-down menu of the AOL places (to 25) that you've visited.

USING AOL'S TOOLBAR

America Online's handy toolbar gives you fast access to all the program's main features, and a quick way to access popular online areas. The toolbar contains 13 icons at the top, as shown in Figure 2.7, each of which represents an online area or command. The second row is used for navigation around the service.

The icons with arrows provide drop-down menus with more features.

FIGURE **2.7** Use AOL's toolbar to activate the program's important features.

Table 2.2 shows all the commands that apply to each toolbar icon.

TABLE **2.2 USING THE TOOLBAR**

ICON	DESTINATION OR FUNCTION
	Top Row
	Check Mail
	Write Mail
	AOL's Mail Center (drop-down menu)
	Print selected document window
	My Files (drop-down menu)
	My AOL (drop-down menu)
	Favorites (drop-down menu)
	Internet (drop-down menu)
	Channels (drop-down menu)
	People (drop-down menu)
	Stock Quotes
	Perks

continues

TABLE 2.2   CONTINUED

ICON	DESTINATION OR FUNCTION
	Top Row
Weather	Weather
	Bottom Row
◁	Previous online area or Web site
▷	Next online area or Web site
⊗	Stop display of Web page
↻	Reload Web page
⌂	AOL's Home Page
Keyword	Keyword menu of recently visited places (drop-down menu)
Find ▾	Go to area entered at left
Go	AOL's Find Central feature

Customize AOL's Toolbar It's easy to add your favorite areas to AOL's toolbar. Just drag a Favorite Place heart to the right end of the toolbar. You see a screen letting you name the item and select artwork for it. When you OK the setting, it's added to the toolbar. To remove the item, Option+Click and drag the tool icon from the toolbar. If your screen is only 800×600, you can use the Option+Click and drag method to remove any of the three icons at the right end of the toolbar to make room for more.

Many of the program features are only available via toolbar commands. Here's a description of the contents of the various toolbar drop-down menus:

- *Mail Center.* This drop-down menu displays various AOL email features. They include email preferences, setting up the Automatic AOL feature, and checking mail received via an automated session.

- *My Files.* This drop-down menu lets you check your online files, such as the messages and files you've downloaded, and modify your personal AOL Web page (this feature is described in more detail in Lesson 12, "Visiting the Internet on AOL").

- *My AOL.* Use this drop-down menu to customize AOL's program features to your taste.

- *Favorites.* This drop-down menu lets you check your list of Favorite Places so you can revisit your favorite online areas.

- *Internet.* This drop-down menu lets you access AOL's Internet features, such as the World Wide Web, FTP, and more. You find more information in Lessons 12 through 14.

- *Channels.* This drop-down menu lets you access AOL's online departments, which cover a number of major interests. You find more information about AOL's Channels in Lesson 3, "Getting Acquainted with AOL."

- *People.* Join an online chat, including a conference featuring your favorites from the worlds of show business, politics, and literature.

 Where's the Rest of the Toolbar? You need a monitor with an 800×600 resolution setting to see all of the toolbar. If your monitor only displays AOL's minimum setting, 640×480, the three toolbar icons at the right won't appear.

In this lesson you learned how to add new local access numbers and set up your AOL software for optimal performance. In the next lesson you visit AOL's online channels, forums, message boards, and software libraries.

LESSON 3

GETTING ACQUAINTED WITH AOL

In this lesson, you receive a brief tour of AOL, visiting many of the most popular online areas. You also learn some convenient keywords to access important features.

VISITING AOL CHANNELS

AOL's Channels are set up much like the channels on your TV set. Choosing one takes you to a specific category of programming. On AOL that sort of programming includes forums (areas where members congregate), message boards, software libraries, chat rooms, and links to the World Wide Web.

When you first log on to AOL, you see the Welcome screen (see Figure 3.1). This screen shows you the major highlights of the service and informs you if you have email waiting to be read.

Why Does the Artwork You See Look Different? AOL updates its look regularly, so the artwork you see displayed for various online areas may change over time. Although the features will be the same, don't be surprised if the artwork for some of the areas you access are different from this book.

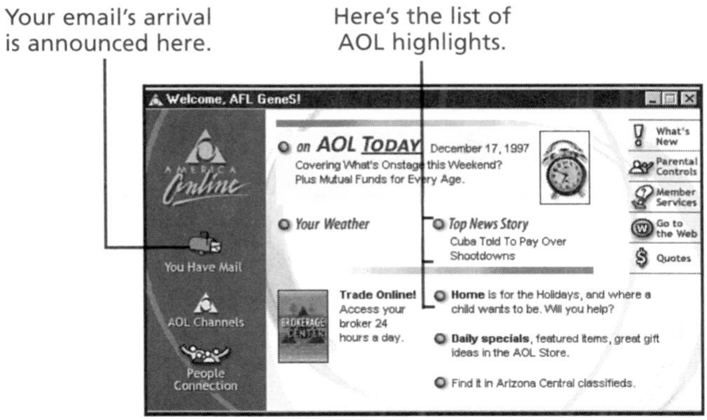

Your email's arrival is announced here.

Here's the list of AOL highlights.

FIGURE 3.1 The Welcome screen shows whether you have email waiting and shows you special features to check out.

All of AOL's popular content areas are available via the Channels screen. (see Figure 3.2). The fastest way to open it is to click the shaded AOL Channels icon at the left side of your Welcome screen.

Click a channel icon to go to online forums devoted to a subject.

FIGURE 3.2 Using the TV metaphor, AOL divides its service into content areas called Channels.

Use Keywords!   You can also reach almost every AOL area by pressing Ctrl+K and typing in the keyword. You can get the full list of keywords via the keyword (naturally) **Keyword.**

Where's that Channel Window?   If you've closed the Channel screen during your online session, you can call it up again by using the keyword **Channels.**

WHERE *Is* IT? USING AOL'S FIND CENTRAL

AOL's Find Central (see Figure 3.3) helps you locate the kind of information or service you want. You can search for AOL forums, Internet information, people, and events, or you can examine AOL's huge software libraries. Just click the topic you want to learn more about it.

Choose the topic to refine your search.

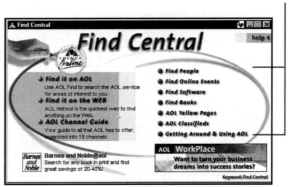

FIGURE 3.3   Find Central helps you locate the area you want to visit on AOL.

Here's a list of AOL's channels you can check out:

- *AOL Today*. This channel (see Figure 3.4) highlights major AOL features and the top news of the day. It's updated often with a listing of "essentials" for you to check further.

Click the label at
the left to call up
another channel.

FIGURE 3.4   A typical AOL channel lists popular online features.

Another Channel Is a Click Away   After you access one AOL channel, you can quickly access it the next time by clicking the appropriate button on the left side of any AOL channel window.

- *News Channel*. This channel offers a vast amount of information about the world today that is as current as it gets. You can read the latest stories from the major wire services, or consult the contents of the major daily newspapers, such as *The New York Times*. You learn more about this area in Lesson 7, "Getting Informed on AOL."

- *Sports Channel.* This channel has the latest sports news, including discussion groups and regular conferences on your favorite sports. You can also converse, through cyberspace, with some of your favorite sports figures. You learn more about this area in Lesson 6, "Getting Entertained on AOL."

- *Influence Channel.* Here's a channel that's devoted to the stories behind the stories, the gossip and intrigue behind world events, and happenings in the world of fashion and show business. You learn more about this area in Lesson 7.

- *Travel Channel.* In this area, you can make travel reservations and get the best prices. You also learn about the best places to visit, where to eat, and what places to avoid. You learn more about this area in Lesson 5, "Shopping on AOL."

- *International Channel.* AOL is not just for the USA anymore; it has expanded into Canada, Europe, Japan, and other major world centers. AOL's International channel lets you quickly access some of AOL's worldwide features.

- *Personal Finance Channel.* This area covers personal finances and the latest business news. You can also check your personal stock portfolio (whether you invest or not). You learn more about this area in Lesson 4, "Doing Business on AOL."

- *WorkPlace Channel.* Whether you work in a home office (as many writers like me do) or run a large business, you can find a wealth of information and special services to consult. You learn more about this area in Lesson 4.

- *Computing Channel.* This channel offers information and help with your PC, some of it direct from the computer makers themselves. You can also find extensive libraries of software for you to download. You learn more about this area in Lesson 15, "Setting Up Automatic AOL Sessions."

- *Research and Learn Channel.* This channel offers online courses, help for students, and virtual visits to major museums around the world, including the Library of Congress and the Smithsonian. You learn more about this area in Lesson 7.

- *Entertainment Channel.* Here's AOL's center for information about movies, television, books, politics, and more. There are also special forums run by the producers of such popular programs as the *Oprah Winfrey Show.* You learn more about this area in Lesson 6.

- *Games Channel.* This area is always popular. Here you can check out the latest CD-ROM games, video games, or one of the thousands of free or shareware games that you can download. You learn more about this area in Lesson 6.

- *Interests Channel.* Join an astronomy, cooking, or photography club or share information about better health and exercise. You'll find all this and more in this convenient online channel.

- *Lifestyles Channel.* What's your goal? Do you want to give up that smoking habit, learn more about physical fitness, or find a perfect mate? Here's the place to seek help. You can find areas devoted to religion and beliefs, and special online communities.

- *Shopping Channel.* Shop at one of AOL's online shopping malls, or visit major stores and companies on the World Wide Web. You can also place your own want ads in AOL's Classifieds area. You learn more about this area in Lesson 5.

- *Health Channel.* Learn about new developments from the world of medicine, or discover new exercise secrets. Or just check an online health guide. You'll find it all here.

- *Families Channel.* AOL prides itself on being "kid safe." This channel takes you to AOL's special features for kids and teens. You also read about AOL's Neighborhood Watch and Parental Controls features, which let you customize the online experience for younger family members. You learn more about this area in Lesson 19, "AOL's Neighborhood Watch."

- *Kids Only Channel.* This area is run strictly for kids. As shown in Figure 3.5, young people have lots of special and friendly places to visit on America Online. You learn more about this area in Lesson 19.

FIGURE 3.5   Here's where kids hang out on AOL.

 Make AOL Safe for Your Kids   You can create a special online experience for your child with AOL's Parental Controls feature (keyword: **Parental Controls**). This feature enables you to restrict your child's access to certain online areas and Internet sources.

- *Local Channel.* Visit the major cities of the USA and the world. This department accesses AOL's Digital City, where you can find information about a specific city, ranging from popular tourist spots to the daily news and messages from local residents.

 How Many Clicks? To access an area shown by an icon, click just once. When your mouse is placed over such an area, you see the cursor change to a hand. To access an area in a text list box, double-click the item (here the cursor doesn't change).

VISITING AN AOL FORUM

AOL's information centers are known as forums. These are places where you can learn about a specific subject, such as personal computing, photography, and more. Each forum has its own roster of news, message boards, chat rooms, and libraries.

A good way to learn how a forum is set up is to visit one. Here, for example, is the PC Help desk (see Figure 3.6). You can reach it via the keyword **PC Help**. This is a great place to get help with your PC, or just learn a few tips to make your online visits more productive.

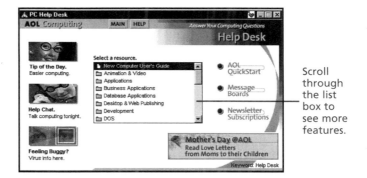

Scroll through the list box to see more features.

FIGURE 3.6   AOL's PC Help forum is dedicated to solving your computer programs as quickly as possible.

 Learn What a Forum Is All About   The first time you visit a forum, look for an icon or list box entry labeled *About* or *About this Forum* (or something similar). By clicking (or double-clicking, as appropriate) the item, you open an information screen that tells you the purpose of the forum and a little about the forum volunteers who run it (AOL calls them "community leaders").

AOL's Online Conferences

AOL features conferences by many famous personalities from show business, politics, and literature. The keyword **AOL Live** will give you the bill of fare. Every feature is a click away, and online conference rooms are easy to reach and fun.

Stop that Screen!   If the text is moving just too fast for you on your PC, or you don't want to read the rest of a text screen, hit the Esc key. That key stops the text from scrolling. But remember, it takes a few seconds for AOL's host computer to get the message, and the text display might be done before it goes into action to stop it.

AOL Keywords You Need

AOL's keywords are the fastest method to get from here to there. Here are ten of the most important AOL keywords you'll want to know:

- **Billing.** If you need to double-check your online bill or change your billing method, visit this area for assistance.

- **Help.** Visit AOL's Member Services area to receive assistance with online problems.

- **Keyword.** Use this area to get the latest list of online keywords (it changes often).

- **Member Directory.** Get a list of fellow AOL members, or make or modify your own online profile here.

- **Members' Choice.** What are the most popular areas on AOL? Members' Choice has the Top 50, so check it out!

- **Names.** You can add up to four additional screen names to your online account. You can use this area to add or remove screen names or change your password. But you cannot change the name you used when you joined the service—your *master* account name.

Switch Screen Names Without Logging Off! If you have more than one screen name on your account, you can switch among them by choosing Switch Screen Names from the Sign Off menu. When you open this feature, check for a dark mail icon to indicate whether there's email waiting on your other screen names. If you haven't stored your password in AOL's software, you'll be asked to enter it before you switch to the other name.

- **Parental Controls.** Create a special, safe environment for your kids on AOL. Depending on their ages, you can limit their access to certain places on AOL and the Internet.

- **QuickStart.** If you're new to AOL, start here and learn how to make your AOL software run at its best.

- **Top Tips.** Visit this area to find the neat tips your fellow members and AOL "community leaders" have found to make your online visit more fun and productive.

- **Upgrade.** From time to time, AOL updates its software to offer new features or better performance. You can find the latest version here. If you want to be on the cutting edge, check the keyword **Preview**, where you often have a chance to download and install a version of AOL's software that hasn't been officially released.

In this lesson, you visited some of the most popular online areas on AOL. You also learned some useful AOL keywords.

LESSON 4

DOING BUSINESS ON AOL

In this lesson, you discover that AOL isn't just a place for fun, it's a place where you can learn valuable information to help run your business better and more profitably.

USING AOL'S WORKPLACE CHANNEL

The center for business information on AOL is the WorkPlace Channel (see Figure 4.1). Another important area for you to visit, AOL's Personal Finance Channel, is covered later in this lesson.

Click here to select another AOL channel.

Your Business center for small business

AOL Business Departments

Business-oriented merchandise

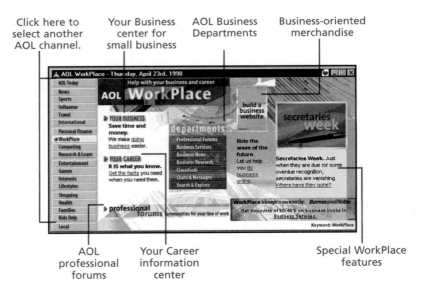

AOL professional forums

Your Career information center

Special WorkPlace features

FIGURE 4.1   Locate business information and receive help and advice at AOL's WorkPlace channel.

Be Careful About the Advice You Get Online! Most business-oriented forums on AOL come with an important disclaimer. The purpose of these areas is to give you information about various aspects of financial management. The forum staff and contributors to those areas are not responsible in any way for the way you use that information to develop and manage your business.

Here's a quick look at the WorkPlace Channel features:

- *Your Business.* A number of forums and information areas where you can learn how to run your business more effectively.

- *Your Career.* Here's AOL's center for advice on helping you advance in your present career or find a new job.

- *Professional Forums.* A number of business categories have special forums on AOL.

- *Products and Services.* AOL offers a number of business-oriented services, such as PrimeHost, a Web hosting service.

- *Business Research.* Consult AOL's own resources and Internet-based databases for the information you need.

- *Classifieds.* Place either free or fee-based ads for your product or service in AOL's Classifieds area.

- *Search & Explore.* You can use AOL's NetFind search engine to check AOL's business-related resources.

USING PRIMEHOST, AOL'S WEB HOSTING SERVICE

AOL's PrimeHost (see Figure 4.2) lets you extend your ability to handle Web commerce. PrimeHost offers an easy way to make a professional Web site, and marketing information to help you get the most from Internet commerce.

Useful Information About Web Commerce   A good source of information about creating and maintaining a Web-based business is Que's *Launching a Business on the Web, Second Edition*. You can find a copy at your favorite book store.

AOL Gives You a Free Web Site Too!   As an AOL member, you can make your own Web site on AOL without extra cost. I'll tell you how in Lesson 12, "Visiting the Internet on AOL." However, this feature has its limits. You only have 2MB of storage space for your Web files, which is okay for a personal site and maybe testing a product, but not enough to give you a full-featured Web site.

Information about
PrimeHost services.

FIGURE **4.2**   PrimeHost is an extra-cost service that lets you take your business to the World Wide Web.

PrimeHost Isn't Free! AOL's PrimeHost service is an extra-cost service. Before you decide whether to use the service, you'll want to consult current pricing and, of course, compare the features to other hosting services to see what meets your business needs.

Using the supplied templates and help information, AOL boasts that you can build your first PrimeHost Web site in 10 minutes flat. But if you want to extend beyond the basic templates, you might want to have a graphic designer customize a Web site to your needs.

 Templates A *template* is basically a document that already has its design elements in place. All you have to do is fill in the necessary information to get a fully formatted document. Your favorite word processing program probably has a similar feature.

USING AOL'S PERSONAL FINANCE CHANNEL

AOL's Personal Finance channel, shown in Figure 4.3, covers financial issues for your business and your personal portfolio too. You can track your stock portfolio, and even get help at tax time.

Click here to select
another AOL channel.

Up-to-date stock
market quotes

The Market
Day forum

Finance channel
departments

Financial
business centers

The latest
financial news

FIGURE 4.3   Money management is the main topic in America
Online's Personal Finance channel.

Some of these Finance Channel features include:

- *Market Today*. AOL provides you with the latest stock market
  information, culled from the major business news services. You
  can also check the latest stock quotes and your investment portfolio.

- *The Markets*. Receive investment tips and track your favorite
  stocks.

- *Business News*. Read the latest stories and informed speculation
  about the future of specific industries.

- *Investment Research*. Before you invest in a company, you can
  get more information here.

- *Investment Forums*. Visit AOL's popular, irreverent Motley Fool
  and other financial information forums by clicking on this area.

- *Investing Basics.* We're not all financial wizards. If you're looking for a route into the maze of confusing and contradictory information about personal finance, this is the area to check out (it's a place I visit often).

- *Advice & Planning.* Receive financial advice and planning assistance here (but remember that AOL's not responsible for the decisions you make with the advice you get).

- *Tax Planning.* Download tax forms and get advice on how to handle your taxes year-round.

- *Personal Finance Live.* Join an online conference on your personal finances.

- *Search.* AOL's NetFind Web-based Search tool is also a great way to locate financial information you need.

- *Mutual Funds.* You can track the progress of your favorite mutual fund here before you invest.

- *Banking.* Many of the largest USA banks offer online banking on AOL.

- *Brokerage.* You can also trade stocks online via one of AOL's stock brokers.

- *Insurance.* You can check out information about the kind of insurance you need and contact online brokers for the lowest prices.

USING AOL'S QUOTES AND PORTFOLIOS FEATURE

AOL's Quotes & Portfolios center (see Figure 4.4) is available 24 hours a day, not just during trading hours.

Type your stock's symbol here
to get an up-to-date quote.

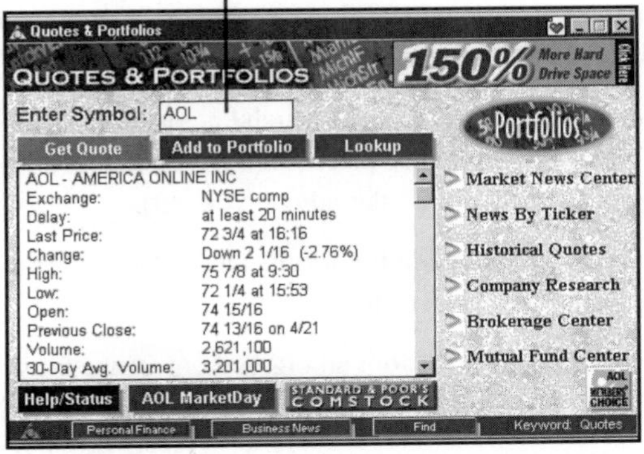

FIGURE 4.4   You can keep your stock portfolio current on AOL.

It's easy to check your stocks on AOL. First enter the stock's symbol
(market entries are usually identified in abbreviated form). You can use
the Lookup Symbol feature to help you quickly find the right symbol. The
Portfolio feature lets you create a custom list of the stocks you own (or
want to consider) and then track their progress.

AOL'S TAX FORUMS

Keyword: **Tax**

AOL's tax forums are designed to provide information that helps you over
some of the hurdles and eases the process of accurately filling out your
tax return. You'll be able to consult the publishers of the major tax software packages (such as Intuit, publishers of MacInTax and TurboTax) and
receive advice from tax experts.

Here's a quick look at AOL's Tax Planning features (see Figure 4.5):

Scroll through the list
box for more offerings.

FIGURE 4.5   AOL's Tax Planning area has valuable information to help you prepare your return as quickly and accurately as possible.

- *Tax News.* Learn about the latest IRS rules and congressional action.

- *Forms and Schedules.* Get tax forms that you can print on your own PC's printer.

Can't Open that Tax Form?   The tax form files you get on AOL (and also the IRS's own Web site) are in Adobe Acrobat format. You can find the program to open and print these forms in AOL's software libraries. See Lesson 15, "Setting Up Automatic AOL Sessions," for information on downloading software from AOL.

- *IRAs and Keogh's.* Receive tips on setting up your personal retirement plan.

- *Tax Software.* Get information about tax software and helpful utilities to make the process of preparing your return easier.

- *On the Web*. AOL offers direct links to the Web sites run by the IRS and private companies.

- *Tax Logic*. You can use AOL's online tax preparation service and have your returns sent electronically direct to the IRS.

- *Tax Help Live*. At tax time, you can consult this area to get fast advice.

In this lesson, you visited AOL's WorkPlace and Personal Finance channels and discovered many of AOL's popular business-related resources.

Lesson 5

Shopping on AOL

In this lesson, you learn about AOL's online shopping center and travel information features.

Visiting AOL's Shopping Channel

America Online's Shopping channel, shown in Figure 5.1, is akin to having a huge shopping mall at your convenience.

Click here to select
another AOL channel.

AOL Shopping Mall's
featured items

Special offers
change daily.

List of offerings
grouped by category

Figure 5.1 Here's where you can shop for the items you want while online.

ORDERING MERCHANDISE FROM AOL

Ordering an item from any of AOL's online shopping areas involves basically the same steps. As an example, let's visit the AOL Store (keyword: **AOL Store**), where you can get custom AOL merchandise such as shirts, jackets, coffee cups, and more.

To see what's available, click the AOL Logo Merchandise icon on the AOL Store screen to open the window shown in Figure 5.2.

Double-click a list box
item to see more choices.

FIGURE 5.2   Pick the kind of item you want to check from the directory.

The picture shows the featured item at the AOL Store. If you want to know more about this item, click the picture and you see a screen similar to Figure 5.3.

 Having Your Billing Information Handy   If you plan on buying something online, have your credit card handy. Or you can just choose to have the purchase billed to the same credit card used for your AOL account (this is the default selection).

Scroll through the text window
to see the entire description.

FIGURE 5.3   The description box contains more information about the product.

Here's how to place your order (the steps may change somewhat when you visit different online merchants):

1. To order the item shown, select the Click Here to Order button.

2. Click Continue to select the item shown on the next screen.

3. Choose the number of items you want.

4. After you've made your selection, AOL confirms your order.

5. Click Review Cart or Shopping Cart (one or the other option will appear on various screens during the ordering process) when you need to recheck your order.

6. To complete your order, click the Checkout button.

7. Enter your billing and shipping information on the next screen (it defaults to your own address and billing information).

Get Free AOL Software Upgrades   AOL updates its software occasionally. If you want the latest, use the keyword **Upgrade** to get information about the new version or download a copy. There's never an extra cost. Sometimes you'll have a chance to download a copy of a new version of AOL software before it's officially released. Use the keyword **Preview** for the latest scoop.

ADVERTISING ON AOL

You can advertise your own items to sell on AOL's Classifieds forum (see Figure 5.4). You have the choice of free ads (bulletin board ads) or fee-based ads, which are fully searchable.

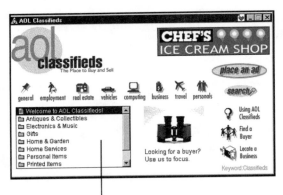

Click the category icon to
see different choices.

FIGURE 5.4   Here's AOL's buy/sell/trade center.

Look Before You Spend!   Before you buy from any online merchant, don't be shy about asking them for some references. It's your money, and you have the right to choose carefully where you spend it.

Before You Shop Online

AOL's online merchants pay premium prices for space on AOL, and they must also provide special service guarantees. But before you make your purchase, consider the following:

- Read the product description thoroughly.

- Read any posted terms and conditions carefully, in case you need to return the product for an exchange or refund for any reason.

- Check shipping charges. Many firms add sales tax to your total price.

- Examine the vendor's forum for information about shipping times (and remember they aren't responsible for delays caused by problems out of their control, such as late delivery of an item to their shipping center).

- Allow enough time for a product to reach its destination if you're buying for a special occasion.

- Make a copy of your order so that you can refer to it later in case you have further questions about the merchandise you ordered.

 Can't Print the Order? Some online order forms consist of multiple text fields, and choosing the Save option in the File menu might not save the complete text of your order. If this is the case, enter the full details of your order in a text document using AOL's memo feature, or use a screen image capture program to record the actual order screen. The Windows Print Screen feature can be a great help here.

- As soon as you get the package, check it for signs of damage. If it appears severely damaged, contact the online vendor immediately for assistance.

- Check the instructions in your package or in the vendor's forum about customer service contacts in case there's a problem.

- Check the warranty information that comes with your purchase. If you need to register it, you need to send in the forms promptly. Remember, warranty service is sometimes performed by an authorized repair center rather than the vendor itself.

- If the firm is not a part of AOL's Shopping channel, a different set of warranties apply, so check carefully.

- It's a good idea to use your credit card for online commerce. If there's a problem, sometimes the credit card issuer can be called on to help.

 Beware of Credit Card Thieves! Shopping on AOL is secured with the latest technology, but you should always guard your credit card and AOL password. Remember that *no AOL employee* will ever ask you online or by email for any of this information. If you get a request for this sort of information, be sure to report it directly to AOL's Community Action Team for action. Use the keyword **Notify AOL** for information on how to report this sort of conduct.

VISITING AOL'S TRAVEL CHANNEL

AOL offers a complete travel reservations and information center by way of its Travel channel (see Figure 5.5).

Click here to switch online channels.   Check your travel plans here.   Special online offers.

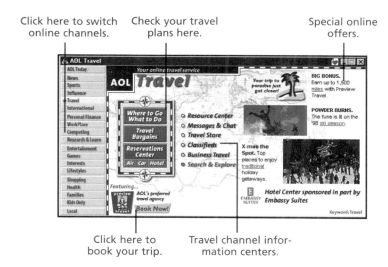

Click here to book your trip.   Travel channel information centers.

FIGURE 5.5   Check AOL's Travel channel before planning a business or vacation trip.

Here's a brief look at the AOL Travel channel:

- *Where to Go, What to Do.* Get the information you need before you decide about places to visit.

- *Travel Bargains.* Find special prices when you book your next vacation or business trip.

- *Reservations Center.* AOL's online travel agencies can help you plan your trip and make flight, car, and hotel reservations.

- *Preview Travel.* AOL has its own online travel service, where you can get the lowest prices before you make your plans.

- *Resource Center.* There's a wide range of information available to help you plan your trip.

Travel Advisories   The world situation is fluid, and some areas of the world may not always be safe to visit. The keyword **Travel Advisories** takes you to an area where you can check the official U.S. State Department travel advisories before traveling to a specific locale.

- *Messages & Chat.* Message boards and chat rooms are always useful sources of information. You learn more about these features in Lesson 10, "Using AOL Message Boards," and Lesson 11, "Joining and Participating in an AOL Chat."

- *Travel Store.* You find special merchandise here, from backpacks to scuba diving gear.

- *Classifieds.* You can place your own buy/sell ads or search for ones that interest you.

- *Business Travel.* This is AOL's resource for planning business trips.

- *Search & Explore.* AOL's NetFind accesses huge database centers to get the information you want as quickly as possible.

What About Connecting to AOL from Your Hotel? Many hotels now offer computer-ready rooms, so you can hook up your laptop computer and go online when you need to. If your hotel doesn't have special rooms for computer users, in some cases, you can remove the cable for the phone from the phone jack and insert your modem cable. Before you do that, make sure the hotel staff won't object.

In this lesson, you learned the secrets of online commerce, and you visited AOL's Travel channel, where you can get information before you plan your next trip.

LESSON 6

GETTING ENTERTAINED ON AOL

In this lesson you learn about AOL's channels that cover the worlds of entertainment, computer games, and sports.

VISITING THE ENTERTAINMENT CHANNEL

Keyword: **Entertainment**

The main screen of AOL's Entertainment channel (see Figure 6.1) introduces you to the sort of entertainment-related content that's available.

Click here to call up another channel.   Your daily Entertainment Spotlight   Your daily Celebrity Fix

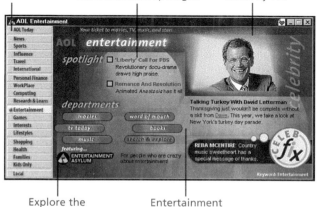

Explore the Entertainment Asylum.   Entertainment channel Departments

FIGURE 6.1 AOL's gateway to information about TV, radio, music, and the movies.

It's Easy to Print the Text You See on AOL!   You can save and print any text document you see on America Online. To print, choose Print from the File menu and okay your printing options before printing. To save the document, choose Save from the File menu.

Some of the features included in the Entertainment channel are

- *Entertainment Spotlight.* Read the latest entertainment headlines and learn about your favorite stars and their current movies or TV shows.

- *Departments.* You'll find forums here for each show business area—even radio.

- *Entertainment Asylum.* AOL's Entertainment channel assembles feature stories and links to popular online features each and every day. And it's highly unpredictable, which explains why it's called an "asylum."

- *Celebrity Fix.* Check out the latest gossip and feature articles about your favorite stars.

Drop-down Menus Deliver More!   Many AOL forums, such as the Movies, Music, and TV Today departments, have a drop-down menu which gives you quick access to additional features.

AOL's Movies Forums

Keyword: **Movies**

AOL's Movies department (see Figure 6.2) is available via a keyword, or simply by choosing Movies at the left side of the Entertainment channel screen.

New movies get special AOL forums.

FIGURE 6.2   Here's an example of the sort of movie-related information you can find each day on AOL.

VISITING AOL'S GAMES CHANNEL

Keyword: **Games**

AOL provides a wealth of resources for fans of computer games, video games, and more (see Figure 6.3).

AOL's Games Insider   AOL's Games Guide   Learn the basics about your favorite games.

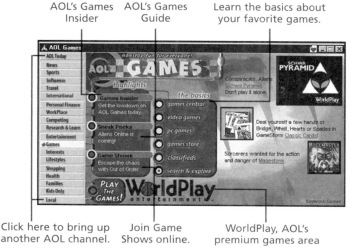

Click here to bring up another AOL channel.   Join Game Shows online.   WorldPlay, AOL's premium games area

FIGURE 6.3   Check out AOL's popular games forums on the Games channel.

What's that Icon Mean? If you don't know what an AOL forum icon (or toolbar icon) means (and sometimes it's hard to tell), just hold the mouse cursor above it. In a second or two, you see a label on the screen showing what the icon represents. This label is known as a ToolTip.

Here's a brief description of some of the AOL Games channel features:

- *Games Insider*. You receive news about special offers, hints, and tips here.

- *Games Guide*. Here's a guide to AOL's online games. Before you sign up, don't forget to check information about premium games (these are extra-cost options).

- *Game Shows Online*. It starts with Trivial Pursuit and covers a whole range of topics. AOL has a lot of interactive games for you to play.

- *Games Central*. Here's where you can discover the hidden secrets behind your favorite games, the sort of material that's not in the manuals.

- *Video Games*. Many of the classic and current video games are discussed here. Plus, you'll find the secret clues that aren't mentioned in the manuals.

- *Computer Games*. Download software, or get updates to your favorite games here. Or just receive some help when you come across a sticking point that's got you stumped.

- *Games Store*. AOL has a fully featured online shopping mall, where you can get good prices on many computer games. See Lesson 5, "Shopping on AOL," for more information about online shopping.

- *Newsstand*. Read your favorite magazines on AOL—often before the printed edition reaches the stands. You find more information about AOL's news and information resources in Lesson 7, "Getting Informed on AOL."

- *Search & Explore*. Access AOL's powerful search engines to find the information you want.

 Not All Online Games Are Free! If you participate in one of AOL's Premium Games, expect to pay an added hourly charge (it was $1.99 per hour when this book was written). Although you should see an onscreen prompt if you enter an area where extra cost services are involved, it's easy to dismiss a warning prompt by mistake if you're in a hurry. You can find more about these special services at the keyword **Premium**.

EXPLORING AOL'S SPORTS CHANNEL

Keyword: **Sports**

AOL's Sports channel (see Figure 6.4) offers the latest sports news, plus your chance to play fantasy games online.

Click here to go to another AOL channel.

Here's AOL's Scoreboard.

Read the latest news and scores.

Check out special featured attractions.

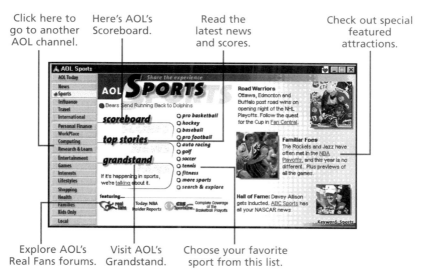

Explore AOL's Real Fans forums.

Visit AOL's Grandstand.

Choose your favorite sport from this list.

FIGURE 6.4   AOL's Sports channel offers news and views and your chance to get involved in a fantasy league.

Some of the features offered in AOL's Sports channel include the following:

- *Scoreboard.* Check the stats and see how your favorite teams and players are doing this season.

- *Top Stories.* AOL brings you information from the major wire services and your favorite papers about the world of sports.

- *Grandstand.* You can get involved in spirited discussions about your favorite sports, and even join a fantasy league, where you can participate in a sport without ever leaving the comfort of your PC (but don't forget, this is an extra-cost option).

- *AOL's Real Fans.* Here's where you really show your dedication to sports. It's a special network of top news and inside information.

- *Choose a Sport.* Which sports do you like? Check out the forums here.

- *Real Fans Sports Network.* If you are truly dedicated to your favorite sports, this forum (see Figure 6.5) is a must-see. You can find the latest news, chats with your favorite athletes, messages from members, and much more.

- *Search & Explore.* Consult AOL's powerful search tools if you can't find the information you want.

 Not All Online Sports Are Free!   If you want to participate in one of AOL's Fantasy Leagues, remember it's not free. For information on the modest charges and how to participate, please check the information text in the various Fantasy Leagues forum areas, which are available at keyword **Grandstand**.

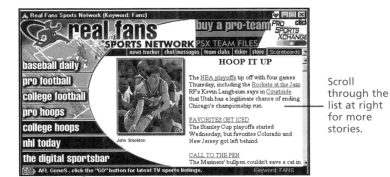

Scroll through the list at right for more stories.

FIGURE 6.5   AOL's Real Fans Sports Network offers the latest sports news, online chats with athletes, and other features.

In this lesson you discovered some of AOL's areas devoted to entertainment, games, and sports.

LESSON 7

GETTING INFORMED ON AOL

In this lesson you discover AOL's vast resources for news, views, and education.

USING AOL'S NEWS CHANNEL

Keyword: **News**

When you log on to AOL, you see the Top News Story of the day on the opening (Welcome) screen. This screen changes regularly, as events occur. You can read major headlines by clicking the Top News Story button, which opens the AOL News screen (see Figure 7.1). This area is organized much like the sections of your daily newspaper.

Check Your Local Weather If you access AOL through a local phone access number (as most members do), you'll see the current Weather displayed in your city on the Welcome screen, labeled Your Weather. To get additional weather information, just click this icon, or click the Weather icon on AOL's toolbar.

The hour's headlines (appear in rotation).　　AOL News departments.

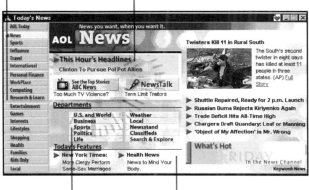

NewsTalk discussions.　　Today's Features.

FIGURE 7.1　Check the latest news from AOL's News channel.

To see a full summary, click This Hour's Headlines, which brings up the screen shown in Figure 7.2. If you want to read the entire story, click an icon labeled More on the Top Stories to locate additional information.

Scroll through the list to see more.

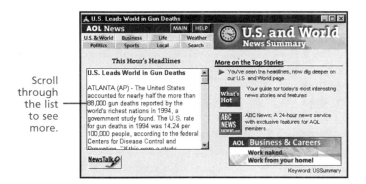

FIGURE 7.2　Here are the hour's top stories from the major wire services.

You can find stories about specific topics of interest under Departments, organized much like your daily newspaper.

See a Slideshow on AOL   When you click the ABC News icon (refer to Figure 7.2), you see a screen where you can view a slideshow, complete with the pictures and sounds of a major story of the day. More presentations are available via the keyword **Slideshows.**

RECEIVE TOP NEWS STORIES AUTOMATICALLY

Keyword: **News Profiles**

AOL's News Profiles feature (see Figure 7.3) lets you receive the latest news on the topics that interest you in your online email box. When you click the Create a Profile button, you are taken through several easy steps to choose topics and news sources, and within hours, you begin to receive the news items that relate to the subjects that interest you.

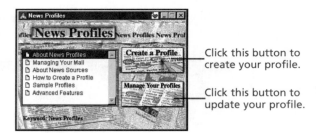

Click this button to create your profile.

Click this button to update your profile.

FIGURE 7.3   Use this feature to receive the latest stories via email.

 Don't Choose Too Many Topics!   Your online mailbox is limited to 550 pieces, and AOL's News Profile sends you a maximum of 50 per day. If you are going to be away from AOL for a while, you'll want to limit the number of new stories that arrive. You can do that by reducing the number of sories selected (by using the News Profile Update feature), or just turn it off until you return to AOL.

READ MAGAZINES AND NEWSPAPERS ONLINE

Keyword: **Newsstand**

Many of your favorite publications have forums on AOL. The keyword **Newsstand** takes you to a listing of many of them. Others are spread throughout the service, in online channels catering to the subject. Such magazines as *Popular Photography* and *Scientific American* and major newspapers such as *The New York Times* offer a large portion of their content, plus special chat rooms and message boards on AOL. You often can check out a new issue before it hits the stands or examine exclusive online reports that never make it to the printed version.

EXPLORING THE INFLUENCE CHANNEL

Keyword: **Influence**

AOL's Influence channel (shown in Figure 7.4) is devoted to the news behind the news. It runs the gamut from information about what your favorite stars are doing to finding out the real stories behind the headlines.

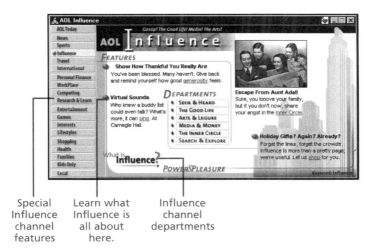

Special Influence channel features

Learn what Influence is all about here.

Influence channel departments

FIGURE 7.4 Learn about the news before it becomes news in AOL's Influence channel.

Here's a quick look at the Influence channel features:

- *Seen & Heard*. This area is devoted to reporting the real truth behind all the gossip you read.

- *The Good Life*. This area is devoted to dining, fashion, and travel to the "in" spots around the world.

- *Arts & Leisure*. Check here to read about new cultural events, including plays, museum exhibits, and books by your favorite authors.

- *Media & Money*. Here you can learn about the movers and shakers in the media from such resources as the Motley Fool and *Business Week*.

- *The Inner Circle*. Here is an area where you can express your own views about what's happening in message boards and chat rooms.

- *Search & Explore*. Consult AOL's powerful research engine to locate the news and views that interest you.

A Brief Look at AOL's Research & Learn Channel

Keyword: **Research & Learn**

Over the years, AOL has become a great resource to do research and to take courses. You can use the Research & Learn channel (shown in Figure 7.5) to consult special databases, online encyclopedias, and other publications, and even take courses in the subjects that interest you.

Fact of   AOL's reference   Pick a subject
the day   resources   to explore.

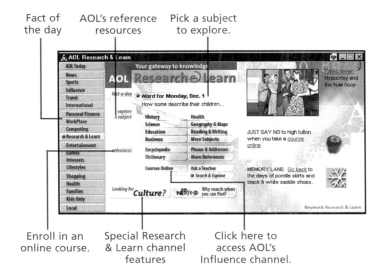

Enroll in an   Special Research   Click here to
online course.   & Learn channel   access AOL's
                features   Influence channel.

FIGURE 7.5   Find information and take degree-granting subjects in the Research & Learn channel.

The Research & Learn channel has the following features:

- *Fact-a-day*. Each day, you read a special quote or learn a special fact about a subject.

- *Explore a Subject*. Consult AOL's database to read something about a specific subject that interests you.

- *References*. Consult phone directories, online encyclopedias, Internet-based databases, and more here.

- *Courses Online*. Your child can get help with homework, and you can take a course from this area.

- *AOL NetFind*. Use AOL's powerful search tools to locate the information resources you want.

Some Online Courses Have a Price Tag! Before you enroll in an online course, check the price. Some of them, available from major educational institutions, include a registration or enrollment fee.

USING AOL'S ASK-A-TEACHER SERVICE

Keywords: **Ask-a-Teacher, Homework Help**

AOL offers a special service that allows students to get the help they need with homework, or to study for a test. The feature is called Ask-A-Teacher (see Figure 7.6).

Choose the grade here to receive help.

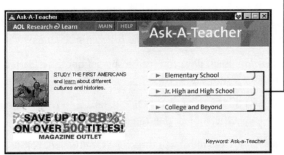

FIGURE **7.6** Ask one of AOL's online instructors to assist you in solving a homework problem.

Here's a brief look at the homework helper features:

- Choose the proper category. You can get help for Elementary School, Jr. High and High School, or College and Beyond.

- When you click the age or school category, you have the option to get help from an AOL instructor by way of the Ask a Teacher feature.

Patience!   AOL's online teachers can be very busy at times, especially when exam time is near. So be patient if your response doesn't come quite as fast as you'd like.

- Consult one of AOL's research tools to find the information.

- Visit an online chat room and talk with an online educator, or leave a message in one of AOL's message boards.

In this lesson you looked briefly at the wide range of information resources available on AOL, by way of its News, Influence, and Research & Learn channels.

LESSON 8

USING AOL EMAIL

In this lesson you learn how to harness the power of AOL's email feature.

HOW TO USE ELECTRONIC MAIL ON AOL

To write email using AOL, simply click the Write icon on the toolbar, or press Ctrl+M. You see the new message screen (see Figure 8.1).

Type your recipient's email address here.

Enter the subject here.

Call out special email features while online.

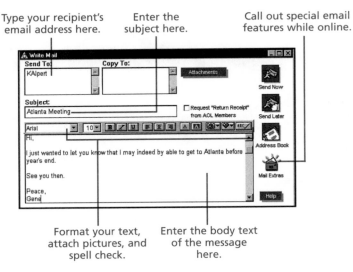

Format your text, attach pictures, and spell check.

Enter the body text of the message here.

FIGURE 8.1   Here's AOL's email form, with all functions clearly labeled.

Use the Tab Key You can use the Tab key to switch text fields in your email form (from recipient, to subject, to message). Alt+Tab reverses the process.

Some things you need to know about preparing email include the following:

- You must include at least one address, a subject, and a message.

- You can send to more than one recipient. Just separate each recipient with a comma or a return.

- To send a copy of the email to another recipient, enter that name in the CC: field at the right.

 Carbon Copies A duplicate copy of the email message usually sent to a third party or parties.

- If you don't want multiple recipients to see who else is getting the message, enclose the name in parentheses. This is a *blind carbon copy.*

- The email address must be entered exactly. There's no room to guess in an online service. Even one incorrect letter or space could send your email to the wrong person.

 Use the Address Book AOL's Address Book lets you keep a handy list of your regular contacts. You learn how later in this lesson.

SENDING EMAIL WITH STYLE

AOL's email is similar to your word processor. You can choose fonts, style, and color. The text formatting toolbar, shown in Figure 8.2, is a convenient way to change type characteristics.

Typeface drop-
down menu

Choose
your style
here.

Pick a text
and back-
ground color.

Click here to add
your Favorite
Place link.

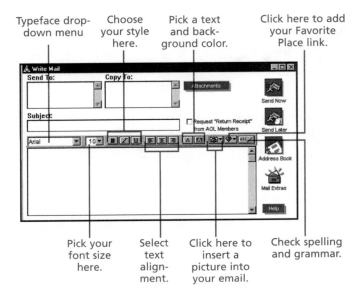

Pick your
font size
here.

Select
text
align-
ment.

Click here to
insert a
picture into
your email.

Check spelling
and grammar.

FIGURE 8.2   Style the text the way you like with AOL's formatting
toolbar.

Don't Overdo Text Formatting!   To have your email
look its best, choose fonts, styles, and color with care.
Too much of a good thing is, well, not so good. And
remember that the recipient of your email needs to
have the same font to see your email the way you set
it up. To send your email to another service (an email
address with an @<domainname> after it), don't bother with formatting. Your fancy text won't transfer to
another service.

SENDING AOL EMAIL

After your email is written and spell checked, just click the Send Now
icon to send it on its way. It will be transferred along with any attachments you've selected. You learn how to attach files later in this lesson.

If you're not logged on to AOL when you write your message, or you don't wish to send it at this time, choose Send Later. The email will be deposited in the Mail Waiting to Be Sent folder when you open the Read Offline Mail screen from the drop-down menu on the Mail Center toolbar.

Send and Receive Email Automatically   AOL's handy Automatic AOL feature lets you send and receive email and message board posts at the times you select. You learn more about this handy feature in Lesson 15, "Setting Up Automatic AOL Sessions."

EMAIL IS NOT JUST FOR TEXT

It's easy to put a picture inside your mail. Just click the camera icon on the email form's formatting toolbar. This opens the Open Image dialog box. Then select the picture file you want to include. It will appear right where you've placed the mouse cursor.

AOL's Picture Gallery feature lets you call up photos from a single screen. You can find the feature in the Edit menu.

Just remember, though: Folks using older versions of AOL's software or who receive your email from another service won't be able to see the pictures you insert. So you might want to consider sending them a picture as an attachment instead (I tell you how a bit later in this lesson).

A Picture Is Worth a Lot of Space!   Another consideration: When you insert pictures in your email, it makes the message a lot larger, so it will take longer to send to your recipient, and longer for the recipient to download the message.

SENDING INTERNET EMAIL

As I explained earlier in this lesson, you can send AOL email to anyone with an online connection, whether they're on AOL or not.

But if the person you want to write to isn't on AOL (which means he can be accessed over the Internet), you have to follow some ground rules:

- An Internet address never contains blank spaces. If someone's mail address has blank spaces, replace them with underscores (_) in the Internet address or just remove the spaces.

- Every Internet address must have the username and domain (location) specified. The username is everything before the @ symbol, and the domain is everything after the @ symbol. An example would be my own Internet address: gsteinberg@earthlink.net.

- Forget about text formatting. I want to repeat this again: The styles you choose with AOL's text formatting toolbar won't translate when the messages leave AOL's boundaries and go to another service.

RECEIVING EMAIL

This part doesn't involve much work on your part. You log on to AOL and see the announcement, You've Got Mail. The icon will also appear on the Welcome screen, as shown in Figure 8.3.

Click here to see your incoming mail.

FIGURE 8.3   You see an announcement that email awaits you on the Welcome screen. The icon is different if there's no mail waiting for you.

When you click the You Have Mail icon (or press Ctrl+R), you see a list of new mail such as the one shown in Figure 8.4. To see the first item, just click once to select it and click the Read icon at the bottom of the list (or double-click the email listing itself), to bring up the first message (see Figure 8.5). From here, use the Next and Prev arrows to move from message to message (if you have more than one).

FIGURE 8.4   Here's your list of waiting email.

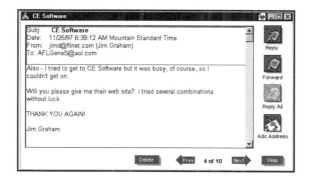

FIGURE 8.5   Here's your email. Click Next or Prev to see another message.

Want to Forward the Message? If you want to send a letter you just received to another online address along with your added comments, use the Forward icon.

After you've read an email message, a check mark will appear next to its title in the New Mail window. Any unread mail will show up the next time you bring up the New Mail window (whether now or on a later AOL session).

Here's how the remaining New Mail features work:

- *Status.* If the recipient is on AOL, here's where you see whether she's read the message or not.

- *Keep as New.* Whether you've read the message or not, this choice flags the message as unread, so it'll show up in the New Mail window next time you check it.

- *Delete.* Removes the message (not only from your list but from AOL's email system), but it also informs the sender (if they're on AOL), that you've deleted it.

- *Help icon.* Click this button to get more help.

ANSWERING EMAIL

It's a good idea to quote a portion of the message you're answering, so the recipient knows precisely what you're writing about. To use the quoting feature:

1. Select the material you want to quote.

2. Click the Reply icon (or Reply All if it goes to more than one recipient).

3. Type your message beneath the quote.

4. If you quote more than one passage, put your response that relates to a segment of the message right below it.

Don't quote too much! You don't need to quote the entire message when replying to it. Just select enough to remind the recipient what you're writing about (usually a few sentences will do).

SENDING EMAIL WITH ATTACHED FILES

If you want to send a file (picture or document) to another member, just click the Attach icon on your email form. You see an Open dialog box where you need to select the file you want to send (see Figures 8.6 and 8.7).

Click the Attach button to select another file.

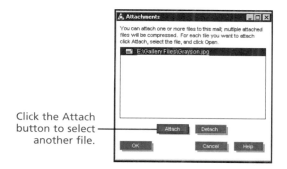

FIGURE **8.6**   The Attach feature lets you connect a file to your email.

Click Open to attach the selected file.

FIGURE **8.7**   Use this dialog box to select the files you want to attach to your email.

When you or your recipient gets email with an attached file, there will be two extra buttons in the received email window, Download File and Download Later. Clicking the Download File button transfers the file from America Online's host to that user's computer. Clicking Download Later marks the file for the Download Manager for transfer at a later time. I tell you more about the Download Manager feature in Lesson 16, "Finding and Downloading Software from AOL."

Be Careful What You Download!   Sad but true: Some folks have been known to send virus-infected files or files designed to extract your personal information from your AOL software or other programs. Virus software cannot detect these files! *It is a not a good idea to download files from someone you don't know.* For more information on handling email with such unknown attachments, use the keyword **TOS** to access AOL's Terms of Service area.

HOW TO SAVE EMAIL

When you've finished reading your email, you have several choices. First, just click the Close box of the email window. The email you've read can be located when you select the Old Mail tab in your online mailbox form. You can always find and read mail you've previously viewed by clicking the Old Mail tab.

Another way to save email is to your Personal Filing Cabinet, a storage place set aside by AOL's software on your computer's drive where you can keep email and other items for later review.

To save an open email message to the Personal Filing Cabinet, simply choose that command from the File menu. You can retrieve this email item at any time, even if you are offline. Your stored email can also be called up from your Incoming Saved Mail drawer (accessible from the Mail Center toolbox icon's drop-down menu).

USING AOL'S ADDRESS BOOK

As you build a list of regular contacts on AOL, you'll want to take advantage of your Address Book, which is your online Rolodex.

Here's how to use the Address Book:

1. Open the Mail Center toolbar icon's drop-down menu and select Address Book, which brings up the Address Book window (see Figure 8.8).

    A blank New Person entry form will appear onscreen.

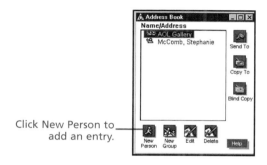

Click New Person to add an entry.

FIGURE 8.8   Place your Address Book entries here.

2. Type the first name of your friend in the appropriate field; for example, **Grayson**.

3. Type the last name of your friend in the appropriate field; for example, **Steinberg**.

4. Type the screen name of your friend in the Email Address field; for example, **Rockoid1**. Be sure you enter it accurately.

5. Place other information about your contact, such as phone number, occupation, or other material, in the Notes field. It won't become part of the email that you address.

6. Click the OK button to save your additions or changes.

To enter more than one recipient in a single category, use the New Group feature instead.

To use your Address Book, just open a new mail window, click the Address Book icon on the right side of the email form, and double-click the name of the person to whom you are sending email. The address will appear in the To window (or the CC window if you choose that option instead).

In this lesson you discovered how easy it is to use AOL's email and Address Book features.

Lesson 9

Using Instant Messages and Instant Messenger

In this lesson you discover how to use Instant Messages for one-on-one contacts with other members, and also how to be informed when your friends or associates are online.

Using AOL Instant Messages

In Lesson 8, "Using AOL Email," you learned how to use AOL email. Email is a great way to communicate with your online friends, but, as with regular "snail" mail (the kind the post office sends), it doesn't allow for fast exchange of information. But if your friends or business contacts are online the same time as you, there's another method that's faster— Instant Messages.

To use this feature, you must be online. To send an instant message, select Instant Message from the drop-down menu on the People toolbar or press Ctrl+I. Either command produces an Instant Message window ready to receive your message (see Figure 9.1).

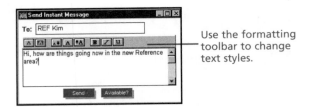

Use the formatting toolbar to change text styles.

FIGURE 9.1   This window appears when you want to originate an Instant Message.

 Keep Your Password and Credit Card Numbers to Yourself   Your online email box and Instant Message windows contain this warning, but I'll mention it again. *AOL staff will never ask you for password or billing information.* If someone claims to be a staff member of AOL and asks for this information, ignore the message! Instead, use the keyword **Notify AOL** to open a form to report the offender. You'll also find a Notify form in Instant Message windows and People Connection chat rooms.

When you get an Instant Message, you can reply by clicking the Respond button, which produces a two-paned window showing the message along with a text screen for your answer (see Figure 9.2).

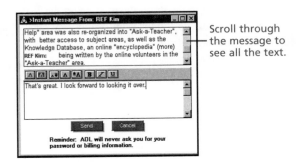

Scroll through the message to see all the text.

FIGURE 9.2   This Instant Message window has space for you to type your response.

Why Aren't They Responding?   Don't be discouraged or insulted if you don't get a response to your Instant Message right away. It's always possible the other member is online, but not seated in front of the computer. If you don't get an answer after a few minutes, just try sending another Instant Message.

To continue the conversation, simply keep the Instant Message window open after you get your response. When messages arrive, you hear a short musical burst on your PC's speaker (if the sound is turned on). You can also hold several Instant Messages conversations at the same time (though sometimes you have to double-check to be sure you're typing your text in the right response window when a new one comes up).

Send Instant Messages via Keyboard   To send an Instant Message via keyboard, simply press Ctrl+Enter rather than clicking the Send button.

You can easily Save or Print the text in your Instant Message window, just like any other text window on AOL.

Why Didn't He See My Message?   If your friend or business associate logs off AOL at the same time your message arrives, he won't see the message. Sometimes you see a response, and sometimes you don't. (It depends on how quickly AOL's host computer network gets the message that the member has just signed off.)

Reducing Window Clutter   If you have several Instant Message conversations going on at once, it's easy to have your screen cluttered with windows. One solution is to choose Cascade from the Window menu of your AOL software. This command groups all the open AOL document windows in a neat row (left to right), one overlapping the other, with the title of each window displayed.

USING INSTANT MESSENGER FOR INTERNET COMMUNICATIONS

Keyword: **Instant Messenger**

An AOL Instant Message is designed strictly for AOL members. But there's a way to have a similar conversation with your friends and colleagues who are members of other services. The feature is called Instant Messenger. To set up this service, you need to invite your colleague to receive and install the software (see Figure 9.3).

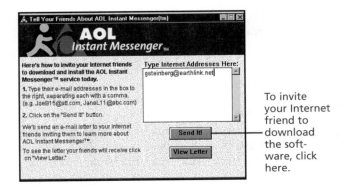

To invite your Internet friend to download the software, click here.

FIGURE 9.3   AOL's Instant Messenger lets you have one-on-one contacts with your friends on other services.

After AOL has the list of friends you want to invite, those friends receive an invitation via email telling them where they can download the software to activate this special feature. After your friend has installed Instant Messenger, she can check to see whether you're online and send you an Instant Message, just as if she were on AOL. And you can keep tabs on her presence online (and whether your other AOL friends are logged on) by way of AOL's Buddy List. You learn more about that feature in the next section.

 There's a Netscape Version Too! Netscape is now offering a version of Instant Messenger at their Web site (http://www.netscape.com), but it's just the same program with a Netscape label attached to it.

USING THE BUDDY LIST

AOL's Buddy List (see Figure 9.4) lets you know when a friend or business acquaintance is online.

The scrolling list shows the screen names your friends use when they are logged on.

FIGURE 9.4   After your Buddy List is set up, it will appear on your PC's screen whenever you connect to AOL.

When you know your friends are online, you can contact them by selecting their name in the Buddy list window, and then clicking the IM button. This produces AOL's Instant Message form, as described in the previous sections of this lesson.

To use a Buddy List, you must first set it up. Type the keyword **Buddy** to produce the setup screen, as shown in Figure 9.5.

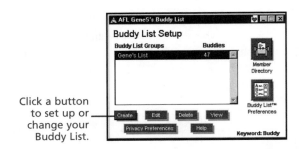

Click a button
to set up or
change your
Buddy List.

FIGURE 9.5   Use this screen to create or update your Buddy List.

To start, click the Create button and type the exact screen names of your
friends in the setup window (see Figure 9.6).

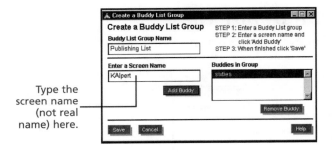

Type the
screen name
(not real
name) here.

FIGURE 9.6   Use this screen to add or remove screen names from
your Buddy List.

You Don't Have to Let Others See You Online!   If
you'd rather not have others put your name on their
Buddy List, click the Privacy Preferences icon, and
choose whether specific members, or any members,
can include you on their Buddy List or contact you via
an Instant Message.

Enter the Right Screen Name! When you set up your Buddy List, use the member's *screen name* (email address), *not* her real name (which might be different). Otherwise, you'll be looking for the wrong person.

If you have more than one screen name on AOL, you have to create a separate Buddy List for each name. You can also create multiple groups, each of which opens a different listing. But the maximum AOL can handle at one time is 50.

Have a Private Chat with Your Friends You can invite your online friends to a private chat. Just click the Buddy Chat icon at the bottom right of your Buddy List screen. Enter the location where your friends should meet in the Location text box and click Send. When your friends receive the message, they click the Go button to enter that online spot. By default, AOL picks a spot for you. You learn more about online chats in Lesson 11, "Joining and Participating in an AOL Chat."

Did You Lose Your Buddy List? It's easy to close the Buddy List window by mistake. To produce it again, use the keyword **BuddyView** or click the My AOL icon on the toolbar and choose View Buddy List from the drop-down menu to bring it up again. Sometimes AOL closes down the feature for maintenance, so don't be surprised if it doesn't show up right away.

FINDING AOL MEMBERS

If you haven't entered a member name on the AOL Buddy List, there's still a way to find out if your friends are online. Just click the People icon on the AOL toolbar and select Locate an AOL Member Online from the drop-down menu, or type Ctrl+L and enter the screen name of the person you want to locate (see Figure 9.7).

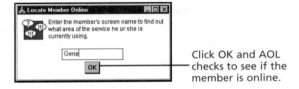

Click OK and AOL checks to see if the member is online.

FIGURE 9.7 To locate a member, enter his or her name in the Locate window.

If your online acquaintance is logged in, AOL displays a screen to that effect. If the person is not online, America Online tells you exactly that.

USING AOL'S MEMBER DIRECTORY

Keyword: **Members**

Another way to find members who share your interests is by way of the Member Directory (see Figure 9.8). To bring up the directory, just choose Search AOL Member Directory from the People toolbar icon's drop-down menu or use the keyword **Members** to bring up the directory screen.

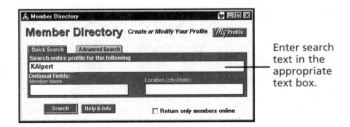

Enter search text in the appropriate text box.

FIGURE 9.8 If AOL members have a profile, you can find them here.

You can locate a member by the real name or the screen name. The
Advanced Search tab opens additional search categories. When a member
is found, you see a screen similar to the one shown in Figure 9.9.

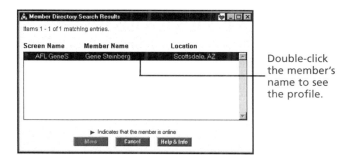

Double-click
the member's
name to see
the profile.

FIGURE 9.9   In this screen, I've managed to locate myself online.

 Why Isn't My Online Friend in the Directory?   In
order for a member to appear in the Member
Directory, he has to make an online profile. Some
members want privacy and remove their profiles, so
don't be surprised if the directory doesn't show them.

In this lesson you discovered how AOL's Instant Message feature can
enhance your communications with fellow members. You also learned
how to set up your personal Buddy List and search through AOL's
Member Directory.

LESSON 10

USING AOL MESSAGE BOARDS

In this lesson you learn how to use AOL's message board feature.

HOW DO MESSAGE BOARDS DIFFER FROM EMAIL?

Here's the main difference between email and message board posts: An email message is designed for a specific individual or group of recipients. Message board posts are public statements, available to anyone who checks. You'll find message boards on AOL cater to lots of subjects, from personal computing to cooking.

In Lesson 8, "Using AOL Email," you learned how AOL's email feature works. Here, I'll show you how to locate the messages that interest you, how to respond to them, and a few of the online traditions governing message boards.

Read Before You Post   The best thing to keep in mind when getting accustomed to AOL's message boards is to look and read before you post. Be sure your message is appropriate to a particular board and covers a similar topic, and please don't post the same message over and over again.

First, you'll want to check AOL's forums for the ones that cover topics that interest you. You'll find AOL's channels are a great starting point (see Lesson 3, "Getting Acquainted with AOL"). For example, if you want to post a message about computers, you'll want to call up the main Computing channel screen, as in Figure 10.1.

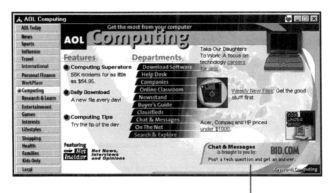

Click the **Chat and Messages** icon
to bring up the topic list.

FIGURE 10.1   Here's AOL's Computing channel.

To check out messages on a specific topic, simply double-click the topic name in the Chat and Messages window, and then examine the topic list for ones that interest you. In the next section I'll cover each message board feature.

HOW MESSAGE BOARDS ARE ORGANIZED

Here's how the message boards are set up:

- *Threaded*. This setup organizes messages by topic.

- *Preference*. This feature lets you sort your messages the way you prefer—oldest, newest, or alphabetically. You can also store your personal online signature.

- *Send an email copy*. This feature lets you send a copy of the message by email to the person to whom you're responding.

- *Offline reading/posting.* You can use Automatic AOL (described in Lesson 15, "Setting Up Automatic AOL Sessions") to read and post messages without being online.

CHECKING MESSAGE BOARD POSTINGS

When you open a message board directory, you'll see a little "post-it" icon next to the title of a message board. In some AOL forums, such areas will be identified simply as Message Boards or Messages. No matter how they're labeled, opening the screen will bring you a directory window similar to that shown in Figure 10.2.

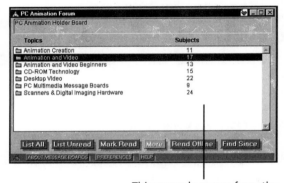

This example comes from the
AOL Computing message area.

FIGURE **10.2**   Typically, a description of its purpose appears at the top of a message board window.

In Figure 10.2, you see the topic or top level of a message board. Sometimes you'll see the second level, or subject level instead.

At the bottom of the window are six buttons, five of which are used to access messages. The options described next always show up in the topic window. Other message board windows group the buttons a bit differently.

- *List All.* Click this button to see the subjects of all the available messages in that message board (at least as far back as you specify in your message board preferences).

- *List Unread.* When you click this button, you'll see a listing of unread subjects in the selected topic folder.

 Use Find Since Instead!   If you are visiting a forum for the first time, choosing this button can produce literally dozens of topic folders and hundreds of messages. You might be better off using the next option, *Find Since* (I'll get to that one shortly).

- *Mark Read.* Clicking the Mark Read button tells AOL's host computer to assume you have read all messages, so it won't display them again. Use this feature with caution.

- *More.* Click the More button to bring up additional entries. If the button is grayed out, there are no more messages.

- *Find Since.* Use this feature to select the timeframe for display of new messages (see Figure 10.3). When you visit a message board for the first time, searching 15 days back is usually enough to bring up a reasonable number of recent messages.

FIGURE **10.3**   Indicate how far you want to search for older messages here.

- *Read Offline.* Select a topic button, then select this button to mark it for offline reading. After a message folder is selected for offline reading, you can retrieve the messages via an Automatic

AOL session (see Lesson 15 for more). Click Read Offline again to unmark the folder. When you use this feature, you'll see a small clock icon to the left of a topic folder when you open the message board again.

 Use Favorite Places! Any AOL screen with the little Favorite Places heart can be added to your Favorite Places directory so you can get to the area again fast. After you click the Favorite Places heart, choose the first option on the acknowledgement screen. To see your personal directory, choose Favorites from the AOL program toolbar.

USING MESSAGE BOARD PREFERENCES

When you click the Preferences button on the bottom of a message board screen, you get the following options:

- *Signature*. Set your default online signature here, up to 256 characters. Use the formatting toolbar to style the signature the way you like.

- *Sort Order*. The normal order is oldest first (chronological). You can set instead to Newest first or Alphabetical. You can always switch preferences around if you don't like them the way they are.

- *Show or download messages posted within the last xx days*. Choose the number of days for which messages are displayed. Usually 15 to 30 days is enough to see recent posts.

- *Download no more than xx messages*. Choose the number of messages that'll be transferred via Automatic AOL. You'll find more about AOL's "automatic pilot" feature in Lesson 15.

VISITING MESSAGE BOARDS FOR THE FIRST TIME

The first time you visit a board, it's a good idea to use the Find Since button. Enter **14** in the In last *xx* Days box, and click Find to bring up the recent message subjects (see Figure 10.4).

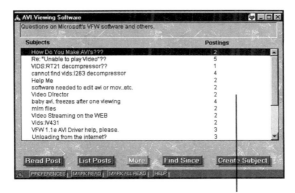

The subjects are shown in
the scrolling list.

FIGURE **10.4**   This screen lists messages by subject.

The bottom of the screen has five buttons you use to find messages to read:

- *Read Post.* Click this icon to bring up the first unread message on a selected subject.

- *List Posts.* Click this to bring up a list of unread messages on a selected subject.

- *More.* If more than 50 items are available, click this button to bring up more messages.

- *Find Since.* This button lets you find recent messages on a selected subject.

- *Create Subject.* Use this option (see Figure 10.5) to make a new subject if you cannot find one more suitable to post your messages (in some forums, this feature is disabled).

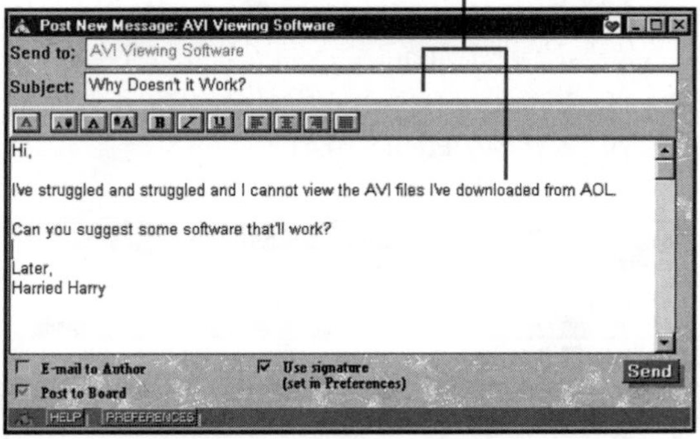

Use the **Tab** key to move from the Subject
text box to the body of the message.

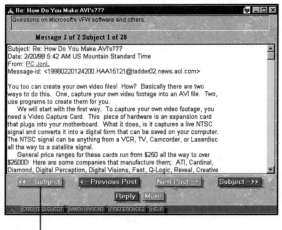

FIGURE 10.5   Use this screen to create a brand-new subject, and
then write your first message about it.

To read your first message, click the Read Post button. You'll see a screen
similar to the one shown in Figure 10.6.

Navigation buttons are grayed out if
no more messages are available.

FIGURE 10.6   This is an example of a typical AOL message board
posting.

Use the Keyboard   When a message is displayed, you can use the arrow keys on your keyboard to move to the next or to a previous posting. To go from one subject to another, hold down the Ctrl and arrow keys. When a navigation button is grayed out, it means no more posts or subjects are available.

To navigate to the next message, click the Next Post button. When it's grayed out, you're at the end of the message thread (or subject). To read the next message thread (message topic folder) click the Subject icon at the right of the screen.

MESSAGE BOARD GROUND RULES

Here are some things to consider before you write your first message on AOL:

- Before you send your message, check it carefully for spelling errors and poor grammar,

- Don't give out personal information. Your message is being posted publicly to an audience of millions of members. *Don't include your address, telephone, or credit card number.*

- Make sure it's relevant. Before you post your message, make sure it's related to the subjects covered in that forum. You wouldn't want to write about cooking, for example, in a forum that covers home theater equipment.

Messages Don't Appear Right Away   After you click Send on a message board screen, it may take a short time before it appears in the message board. The message isn't being checked by anyone; it just takes time for AOL's host computers to process the message and add it to the board. There is, though, a staff of AOL community leaders who will routinely check a message board for older messages or those that violate AOL's Terms of Service (so be nice online).

HOW TO POST A MESSAGE

If you see a message you'd like to answer, click the Reply button
(see Figure 10.7). This button brings up a Post Response window, which
looks like the one shown in Figure 10.7. You'll see the subject line is
already filled in with the subject of the message to which you're responding.

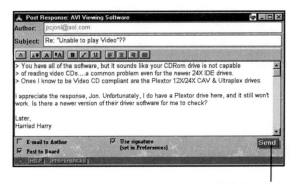

Click **Send** to post your
new message.

FIGURE 10.7   Write your response on this screen.

Before you send your message, you may want to consider the options:

- *Email to Author.* Check this option to send a copy of the message to the author of the one you're answering.

- *Post to Board.* This is the default setting. It adds your message to
  the message board.

- *Use signature (set in Preferences).* This is the signature you set
  as a message board preference.

Don't Forget to Sign It!   It's considered good online
practice to sign your messages, just as it's good online
practice to sign your email.

Reviewing Online Etiquette

Here are a few things to consider before you write a new message:

- *Read before you post.* Check past messages in case your questions have already been answered by another member.

- *Consider your audience.* You are posting a public message here, accessible by an audience that may number in the millions. If you wish to contact just one person, sending email may be a better idea.

- *Show respect and be polite when you post a message.* Don't get personal. If you disagree with someone, talk about the issues, and don't attack someone personally, even if his comments made you angry. And remember it's against AOL's Terms of Service to insult or harass other members or use vulgar language.

- *When responding, quote as necessary.* When you reply to a message, quote the relevant portions of that message at the beginning of your response, or before each part of your response that refers to that message. Don't quote the entire message (it wastes a lot of space). It's standard online form to use the forward sign (>), as a quotation mark, at the beginning of each line, as shown in the following example:

  > I really don't understand what the big fuss

  > over the new Tom Hanks movie is all about.

  > I thought Philadelphia was a much better

  > flick.

- *Be brief.* Don't try to write your great American novel. Just be clear and to the point. At most you can write only a few hundred words in a message board screen, and, when you get a message that there's no more room, it means your message is probably too long.

- *Watch out for the copyright.* Don't use copyrighted material without permission of the author or publisher. You can, though, quote a few sentences from a copyrighted work when commenting on it. This is considered "fair use."

WHERE'S THE RESPONSE?

Don't expect a response right away. Folks log on to AOL at various times of the day, and members who might be interested in responding to your message may not be online immediately. So be patient.

 Make a Message Board Log   AOL's Log Manager (click the My Files icon on the toolbar and select it from the drop-down menu) can be used to make a text record of a message board. Just use the option to make a System Log. Once the log is open, open the message boards and navigate through the messages you want to save. If you've already seen the messages, you have to use the Find Since feature to display them a second time. Just close the log when you're done.

Use the List Unread feature in the forum's message window to see the messages posted since the last time you logged on.

In this lesson you learned how AOL's message boards are set up and how to use them for best advantage.

LESSON 11

JOINING AND PARTICIPATING IN AN AOL CHAT

In this lesson you discover the fun and excitement of online chatting.

USING AOL'S ONLINE CHAT FEATURE

At any time of the day or night, there are dozens of virtual rooms and auditoriums open and active on AOL. That's where online chats are held, and the audience might consist of a handful of folks or, when show biz personalities are around, the audience might number in the thousands.

WHAT'S A CHAT AND WHAT'S A CONFERENCE?

A virtual room is a small place, the online equivalent of a chat room. Depending on how it's organized, it can hold either 23 or 48 members. If more members try to get in, a second room is created.

A conference room is more like a regular auditorium and it's structured to hold an audience that can number in the thousands.

ENTERING A CHAT ROOM

To start chatting, choose Chat Now from the People drop-down menu on your AOL program toolbar. As shown in Figure 11.1, you are taken directly to a People Connection Town Square.

Screen names of those
present at the chat.

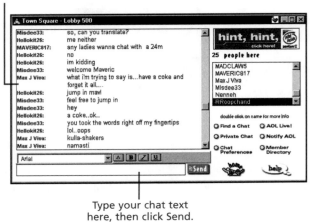

Type your chat text
here, then click Send.

FIGURE 11.1   AOL's Town Square is the first room you enter when
you want to chat on AOL.

Chatting with another member is easy. Just type your comment in the
small text box at the bottom of the chat room window. To post your comment, click the Send button or press Enter.

Look Before You "Speak"!   Before making a comment, it's a good idea to just hang out and see what
other folks are talking about. And when you're ready
to "talk," show good manners and wait for someone
else to finish before sending your comment.

Here's a look at the other features on the chat room screen:

- *People Here*. Here are the people present at the chat. When you
  double-click anyone's name, you see a screen that lets you send
  them an Instant Message, check their online Profile, or, if they're
  being rude, ignore them completely.

- *Find a Chat*. Click here to bring up a list of other online chats in
  progress.

- *Private Chat*. Click here to create a private chat room. When a room name is made, you can invite your friends to join you there for a private talk.

- *Chat Preferences*. Click here to set several preferences, such as whether names in the People Here directory are listed alphabetically or in the order in which the member joins the chat.

- *AOL Live!* You find a list of upcoming online conferences by clicking this icon. You learn more later in this lesson.

- *Notify AOL*. If another member is annoying you or becoming obnoxious in a chat room, you can report the problem by clicking this icon and following the instructions on the next screen.

- *Member Directory*. You find more information on how to use AOL's Member Directory in Lesson 9, "Using Instant Messages and Instant Messenger."

ATTENDING ONLINE CONFERENCES

Keywords: **Live, AOL Live**

Large-scale events are much too much for a small chat room. AOL has created a special auditorium where such events are held. You can find news about those conferences in AOL Live (see Figure 11.2). At any time of the day or night, several large meetings may be in progress.

Click a picture to learn more about the event.

FIGURE **11.2**   You can meet famous personalities in an AOL Live conference room.

Don't Forget to Use Help!   If you find yourself lost in a conference room, just check for the Help button to get online assistance.

 Check for Conference Logs   Don't worry if you miss a conference. The Event Transcripts button on the AOL Live screen is a handy place where you can usually find a log from a recent conference. If you need help downloading a transcript file, check out Lesson 16, "Finding and Downloading Software from AOL."

HOW TO PARTICIPATE IN AN ONLINE CONFERENCE

When you've found a conference you want to attend, click the icon advertising the event to get to the auditorium (see Figure 11.3).

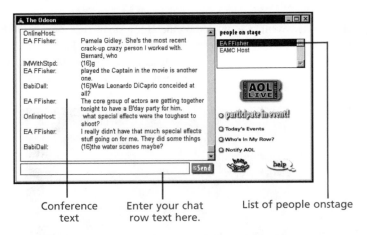

Conference text   Enter your chat row text here.   List of people onstage

FIGURE 11.3   Here's an AOL Live conference already in progress.

In addition to seeing the conference text in the window, you also see the comments made by the folks in your row. If you find that distracting, you can turn off the row chat feature. Just click the Who's in My Row icon shown in the conference room window. Then click the Turn Chat Off button in the window that appears. From here on you won't be disturbed by any chats going on in your row.

If you want to move to another seat, click the Other Rows button, select the row you want to enter, and click the Switch Rows button. Because chat rows are each limited to eight members (16 members in some larger conference rooms), you won't be able to enter a row that's already filled.

If you want to get involved in the conference, click the Participate in Event icon in the main conference room window (see Figure 11.4), and then type your statement. Click the appropriate button to indicate whether you're sending a comment or question. The Vote and Bid buttons are meant for special online contests.

Ask a conference guest a question or make a comment.

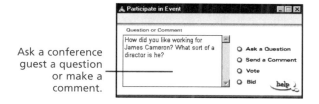

FIGURE 11.4   Type your question for the conference guest here.

Was Your Question Ignored?   Some of the conferences featuring famous show business and political figures get an audience in the thousands. There's no way to answer all the questions, so the host will pick a few. Sometimes you'll be able to email the guest with more questions—but usually the guest's AOL screen name is temporary. It's just used for the conference and will be deleted after the session is over (so they won't be able to get mail from you).

HOW TO BEHAVE IN A CHAT ROOM

As with message boards and email, AOL expects you to behave responsibly in a chat. Here are the basics:

- *Watch your language.* Vulgar language isn't allowed, even if the chat seems to get out of control or you get angry over something that was said.

- *Don't interrupt.* As in regular conversation, wait till someone's finished before you "talk" (send your comment). And consider this when making your own comments:

    Use ellipses (…) to signify that the statement isn't yet finished, and more text is to be added.

    Use the words "go ahead" or the initials GA to indicate that you've finished your statement (and please be brief).

- *Avoid irrelevant topics.* If it isn't an open topic chat, be sure to confine your comments to the subject under discussion.

A BRIEF DESCRIPTION OF CHAT PROTOCOL

Many chats are set up with "chat protocol" to keep the flow of conversation smooth and prevent unnecessary interruptions. Here's how it works:

- Type ? in the chat window if you have a question.
- Type ! in the chat window if you have a comment about the topic being discussed.
- Wait until the chat host calls on you before you make your comment (even if you're next).

ONLINE SHORTHAND

Because you can't see the person you're talking to online, a series of keyboard abbreviations has been set up to show emotion. They're called *smileys* or *emoticons*.

Some of the more popular smileys include the following:

Abbreviation	Stands For
LOL	Laughing Out Loud
ROFL or ROTFL	Rolling On The Floor Laughing
AFK	Away From Keyboard
BAK	Back At Keyboard
BRB	Be Right Back
OIC	Oh, I See
IMO	In My Opinion
IMHO	In My Humble Opinion or In My Honest Opinion
TTFN	Ta-Ta For Now
TTYL	Talk To You Later
GMTA	Great Minds Think Alike
IHTBHWYG	It's Hard To Be Humble When You're Great
<g>	Grin
GA	Go Ahead

In this lesson you discovered the secrets of online chatting and attending online conferences. You also got a fast tutorial on common online abbreviations.

LESSON 12

VISITING THE INTERNET ON AOL

In this lesson you learn about AOL's Internet services.

USING AOL'S INTERNET FEATURES

AOL integrates Internet access throughout the service. You don't have to learn anything special to use these features. They're built in to the AOL software you've already installed.

AOL'S INTERNET SERVICES

Keyword: **Internet**

A quick way to access AOL's Internet-based services is through the Internet Connection (see Figure 12.1). From here you can check out each feature and find some useful tutorials on how to make them work at their best.

When you click the Internet Extras button (shown in Figure 12.1), you see more features, as illustrated in Figure 12.2.

Access AOL's
NetFind search
feature.

Go to the
World
Wide Web.

Newsgroup
message
center

Timesaver tips
to speed up
Internet
performance

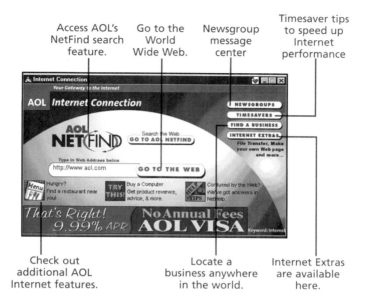

Check out
additional AOL
Internet features.

Locate a
business anywhere
in the world.

Internet Extras
are available
here.

FIGURE 12.1 You'll find AOL's Internet services conveniently grouped in one location.

Use FTP to
download
software.

Use Gopher
to find
information.

Personal
Publisher for
Web pages

Get
Internet
Help.

Download
Internet
Software.

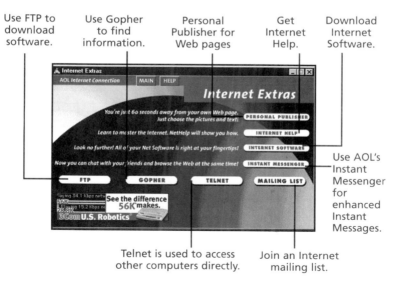

Use AOL's
Instant
Messenger
for
enhanced
Instant
Messages.

Telnet is used to access
other computers directly.

Join an Internet
mailing list.

FIGURE 12.2 AOL's Internet Extras provide a full range of features plus instruction material.

In the next few sections, I cover some of these features in more detail.

USING AOL'S WEB BROWSER

Keyword: **WWW**

With AOL, the Web browser is integrated into the software, so you'll often call it up when you access a specific forum or feature. When you do, you'll see a Web page just as shown in Figure 12.3.

Click an icon or underlined
title to see more pages.

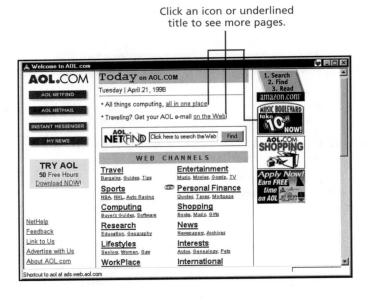

FIGURE **12.3**   This Web page is AOL's.

Navigating through a Web page is easy. Just click an underlined title or icon to bring up more pages. The mouse cursor changes to a hand when you're pointing it at the right place. Or use the scrollbars to see the rest of the page on the screen.

Web sites are also identified by their address, or URL (short for "uniform resource locator"). That's the stuff that follows the *http://* prefix. You'll often find the URL listed on a company's stationery, business cards, and even on their TV ads.

USING AOL'S NEWSGROUP FEATURE

Keyword: **Newsgroups**

An Internet newsgroup (also known as Usenet) is set up similar to an
AOL message board, only it's shared across the entire Internet (see
Figure 12.4).

Click **Read My Newsgroups**
to see the latest messages.

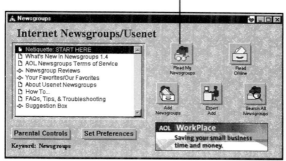

FIGURE **12.4**   Thousands of newsgroups are available from AOL.

When you call up the Newsgroups area for the first time, you find some
newsgroups already selected for you, when you click the Read My
Newsgroups icon. To see more newsgroups, just do the following:

1. Click the Add Newsgroups icon to bring up a listing of newsgroups.

2. Scroll through the list to find the topics that interest you.

3. Double-click a topic to bring up the listing of available newsgroups.

4. Double-click a newsgroup title that you're curious about.

5. Click the Add button to subscribe to that group, which adds it to
   the list shown under the Read My Newsgroups icon.

6. If you'd like to read newsgroup messages offline, click the Read
   Offline icon (shown in Figure 12.4) and Add the newsgroup title
   you want to include in your Automatic AOL Session. I tell you

more about Automatic AOL in Lesson 15, "Setting Up Automatic AOL Sessions."

7. If you decide you aren't interested in a newsgroup after you've subscribed to it, no problem. Just click the Remove button in the Read My Newsgroups screen to take it off your list.

 Don't Add Too Many Newsgroups!   An Internet newsgroup might contain hundreds of messages each day. If you add too many at once, you might find yourself inundated with unread messages to check. It's a good idea to add just one or two at a time, and get up to speed on what information they provide before moving on. You can always remove a newsgroup if it doesn't interest you.

TRANSFERRING FILES ON THE INTERNET

Keyword: **FTP**

In Lesson 16, "Finding and Downloading Software from AOL," you discover how to access one of the thousands of software libraries on AOL. But there's lots more, and AOL's FTP feature (see Figure 12.5) has it for you. FTP (short for "file transfer protocol") is the method used to transfer files across the Internet.

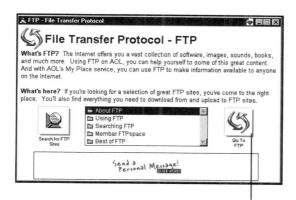

Click Go To FTP to see
AOL's Favorite Sites.

FIGURE 12.5   Access thousands of software libraries from AOL.

The Go To FTP icon is a fast way to get used to FTP. It opens a list of
popular sites selected by AOL, such as Microsoft and others.

FINDING INFORMATION ON THE INTERNET

Keyword: **NetFind**

There's no way to begin to catalog the large amount of information available from the Internet. So much is out there that you seldom know where
to look. AOL has a special feature, NetFind, that helps you locate the
items you want.

More Ways to Search for Material   Another convenient method to locate information is AOL's Gopher
feature (see Figure 12.6), which is accessed with the
keyword **Gopher**.

FIGURE 12.6   AOL's Gopher feature lets you tap lots of information resources.

USING AOL'S MAILING LIST FEATURE

Keyword: **Mailing Lists**

Another convenient way to keep abreast of exciting discussions is through an Internet mailing list (see Figure 12.7). A mailing list lets you receive all the messages via email, right to your AOL mailbox.

Click here to check
    the listings.

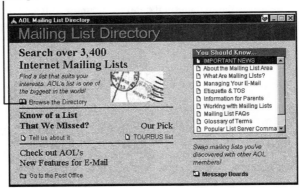

FIGURE 12.7   It's easy to join a mailing list on AOL.

USING AOL'S BRING YOUR OWN ACCESS PLAN

You may already have an Internet account, from a service such as AT&T WorldNet, EarthLink, Netcom, or a similar firm. And you don't have to give that up to join AOL. You can use both, and AOL will give you a cheaper price if you do, using its "bring your own access plan." You learn more about this account option by the keyword **Billing.**

AOL AND INTERNET PROVIDERS— WHAT'S THE DIFFERENCE?

Some Internet providers like to tell you that AOL is an entry-level service, and when you're ready to sign up for the "real thing," you'll join them instead.

But actually there are very distinct differences between AOL and the Internet service (or ISP for short). As you've seen in this book, AOL has literally thousands of forums, containing information, software libraries, message boards, and chat rooms. These features are only available to AOL members and nobody else. An ISP, on the other hand, gives you a connection to the Internet and not much more (except, perhaps, for a fancy "Home" or introductory page with quick access to a few features). The "bring your own access" billing plan that AOL offers lets you get the best of both worlds: the efficient ISP connection (which helps you avoid some of the busy signals AOL's own network is known for), plus all the AOL content that you want.

HOW TO CONNECT TO AOL VIA AN ISP

If you have an ISP connection already, it's easy to log on to AOL as part of that connection. You just have to set up a TCP/IP location in AOL's software. Here's how:

1. Open AOL's software, but don't log on.

2. Click Setup on your AOL software's opening screen.

3. Click the Add Location button to bring up a Setup screen.

4. In the Add Location dialog box, give your setup a name (TCP/IP
    is fine). Choose the option labeled Add a Custom Connection
    (for example, TCP/IP). Then click the Next arrow at the right.

5. Name your connection profile as you see fit. If you're using a
    regular Internet provider and not doing a special connection
    through an office network, leave the default setting, Automatic
    Connection Script: Direct TCP/IP Connection, selected.

6. Click the OK button to put your settings in effect. If you need a
    special setting, you might want to contact your network adminis-
    trator for further assistance.

7. To activate your TCP/IP settings, choose that option from the
    Select Location drop-down menu on your AOL Sign-On screen.

After you've set up AOL's software with a TCP/IP option, here's how to
connect via your ISP:

1. Log on to your ISP in the usual fashion.

2. When you're connected, open your AOL software, and sign on.

3. When your AOL connection is finished, sign off AOL, then dis-
    connect from your Internet provider.

In this lesson you discovered AOL's Internet features and learned how to
connect to AOL via your Internet service provider.

LESSON 13

MAKING WEB PAGES IN AN INSTANT

In this lesson you learn how to make your own Home Page on the World Wide Web in five minutes flat!

As an AOL member you have a total of two megabytes of storage space on AOL's computer network. You can use that space to store your personal files (via AOL's FTP feature, discussed in the previous lesson), but the best way to use it is to create your own personal page on the World Wide Web.

You can use your Web page for fun, to tell your friends about yourself, to post your personal thoughts and photos, or you can use it to promote your business.

BEFORE YOU START

Personal Publisher is a great way to get your feet wet. You can create a professional quality Web page in minutes, but the options are simple. There's a handful of stock pictures to choose a few background templates from. Nothing complex. And you can add your own photos and artwork too. If you decide you really want to make a complex Web page, or you've already had experience doing so, you may want to consider *AOLpress*, AOL's own no-cost Web authoring software. You can get the latest version via keyword **AOLpress**. You can also create great Web pages with such programs as Microsoft's FrontPage and Netscape Composer.

Keep Pictures Small The bigger the picture, the larger the file, and the longer it takes to appear onscreen. The best suggestion is to save your personal artwork in JPEG format (your image processing or scanning software can usually do this) to reduce file size and keep quality high.

USING AOL'S PERSONAL PUBLISHER

Keywords: **My Home Page** or **Personal Publisher**

AOL makes it real easy to prepare your Web page. You don't have to know how to handle codes or special software. AOL takes you step-by-step through the process.

To access Personal Publisher, click the My AOL icon on the toolbar and choose Personal Publisher from the drop-down menu. You can also use the keywords. Whichever method you choose, you see the screen shown in Figure 13.1.

Scroll through the list
to see more choices.

FIGURE **13.1** Here's the first step toward making your own personal Web page on AOL.

These Screens May Change!   The instructions shown here are based on version 2 of AOL's Personal Publisher software. As this book was written, AOL was working on a new version that will offer many of the same features, but in a different form. So if things look different when you try to make your Web page on AOL, just follow the online instructions carefully, using this book as a guide to what sort of material to add, and you'll do just fine.

CHOOSING A TEMPLATE

When you click the Create a Page option in the screen shown in Figure 13.1, you have several choices to get the process started. A good first step is to pick a template (see Figure 13.2). A template sets up the layout of your Web page.

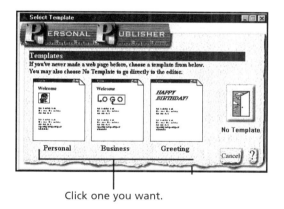

Click one you want.

FIGURE **13.2**   Pick a template for your Web page.

What Kinds of Templates Are There?   AOL's templates are clearly marked as to their purpose, with an illustration of the basic layout. The designs cover Personal, Business, and Greeting. If you don't like them, choose No Template and design the page the way you like.

After you find a template you want, double-click the title to move to the next screen. Don't worry if you're not sure that it's the right one; you can always change it later.

WRITING A TITLE AND HEADLINE

Now that you've picked a template, you'll want to give your page a title and headline (see Figure 13.3).

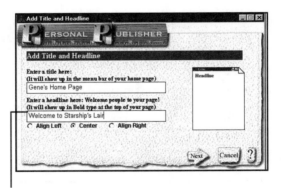

Use the Tab key to go to the next text box.

FIGURE 13.3   After you type your title and headline, click Next to continue.

ADDING BACKGROUND ARTWORK

After your Web page is titled, you can pick a background color or text to enhance its look. You can choose not to have a special background color, leave it white and move to the next design feature, or select an image or color (see Figure 13.4).

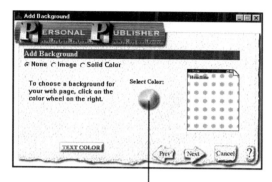

Click the color wheel to see your choices.

FIGURE 13.4   You can see a preview of how the artwork looks by double-clicking its title.

ADDING PICTURES TO YOUR PAGE

AOL gives you some clip art to enhance the look of your Web page (see Figure 13.5). All you have to do is double-click the item's title to see what it looks like.

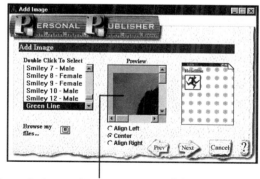

Scroll through the preview to see more of the picture.

FIGURE 13.5   Use AOL's own clip art, or pick one of your own pictures.

AOL's software libraries have a good selection of clip art to use. The keyword **PC Graphics** takes you right to the forum that handles this sort of material. You can also use your own artwork or personal photos. To add one of your own files, just click the Browse My Files icon and select the file you want to transfer to your Web page from your PC's drive.

 Watch Out for Copyrighted Material!   When you buy a collection of clip art, you usually have the right to use it as you want. The same is true for clip art in AOL's software libraries, or your personal photos. But if you want to add any other picture, you need to check with the copyright holder (publisher or artist) to see if it's all right.

ADDING TEXT

After the artwork has been selected, it's time to type your message (see Figure 13.6). The first option is designed for personal information. See Figure 13.7 for more text entry choices.

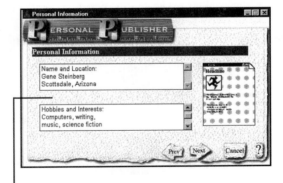

Use the Tab key to go
to the next text box.

FIGURE **13.6** Type your personal information here.

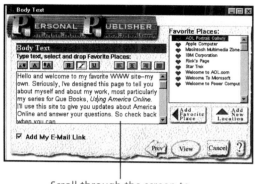

Scroll through the screen to
read the entire message.

FIGURE 13.7   Place your personal message in this text box.

Your text can include personal information about yourself, your background, your interests, whatever you like. Just remember that AOL's Terms of Service apply here too, so watch your language.

 Spell Check!   Don't forget to check the spelling of your message before you're done. Poor spelling and grammar reflect poorly on you.

DONE YET?

We're now at the finish line. When you've finished setting up your Web page, you'll want to see what it looks like. Click the View button to open the screen shown in Figure 13.8.

Scroll through the
page to see it all.

FIGURE 13.8   Check your Web page before you post it.

If you're still not satisfied with your Web page, click the Edit button to make further changes.

When you're finished, click the Publish button in the viewing window to complete the process. You see an onscreen progress bar showing the transfer of the contents of your Web page from your computer's drive to your personal FTP site. This is where AOL stores the page.

You'll see the URL (the Web address) so you can send it to your online friends for fast retrieval later on.

WHERE'S THAT PAGE?

To view your web page, or access one belonging to another member, use this URL: http://members.aol.com/<screen name>.html.

If you're not sure whether a member has such a page, use this URL: http://members.aol.com/. A document window appears in which you can enter the screen name of the person whose page you're trying to find.

WEB SERVICE FOR BUSINESSES

Your Personal Publisher Web site is fine as an introduction. But if you want to promote your business, you'll find it has limits. One of those restrictions is the two megabyte storage space, which limits the number of pictures you can add, and the number of additional pages you can make.

If you decide you'd like to build a professional Web site for your business, check with AOL's custom hosting service, at keyword **PrimeHost,** for more information. It is an extra cost service, and the prices are spelled out when you visit that area.

Shop Around!   You might want to examine the Web hosting services performed by some of the dedicated Internet providers before deciding whether to use AOL. Some companies also offer design services. Pricing varies, depending on how much traffic you expect and how elaborate the site will be. As with any service, it's never a bad idea to shop around.

In this lesson, you discovered how AOL's Personal Publisher lets you build your own Web site in minutes.

LESSON 14

USING OTHER
INTERNET
SOFTWARE WITH
AOL

*In this lesson you discover how easy it is to run other Internet programs
such as Netscape, as part of your AOL connection.*

YOU'RE NOT STUCK WITH AOL'S
OWN WEB BROWSER

AOL offers a full suite of Internet features you can use without any other
program. You can browse the World Wide Web, get files via FTP, access
Internet newsgroups, and more.

But that doesn't mean you can't use other Internet programs if you prefer.
AOL uses Microsoft's Internet Explorer as its Web browser (it just opens
Web pages in AOL's own special window). If you're used to Netscape for
Web surfing, for example, you can still use it as part of your AOL connec-
tion.

Lost Your Internet Access? You need to be logged
on to AOL to use its Internet features. If you suddenly
get disconnected, you'll find that other Internet software you've run as part of your AOL connection will
stop running. The solution is to log on again.

To use Netscape as part of your AOL connection, just log on to AOL, and then launch Netscape normally, which brings up Netscape's browser screen (as shown in Figure 14.1).

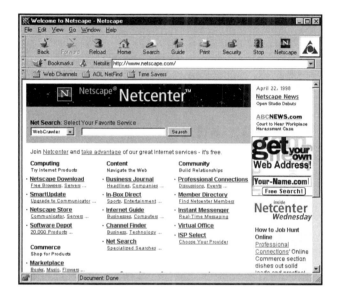

FIGURE 14.1 Yes, you can use Netscape while on AOL.

 The AOL-savvy Version of Netscape Netscape has created a special version of its Navigator browser designed to work best with AOL. To get your copy, use the keyword **Netscape** and move over to the download area. Of course, if you already have Netscape installed, there's no reason you cannot continue to use it and get good performance (although the AOL version might be a little faster because it connects directly to AOL's own Web servers).

When you're finished using Netscape, just exit the program in the usual fashion (choosing Quit from the File menu), and then log off AOL.

A Cool Way to Speed Up Internet Access   Connectix
Surf Express is a program designed to speed up Web
performance. It works with both Internet Explorer and
Netscape. It works best when you access the same
Web sites regularly; the publisher claims performance
is boosted up to 30 times. You can download a
demonstration version from the Connectix AOL forum
at keyword **Connectix**.

THE LIMITS OF USING OTHER NET SOFTWARE

AOL has a special link to its own browser, programmed into the software.
So while you can run Netscape (or even a different version of Microsoft
Internet Explorer than is provided by AOL), there are some limits:

- *Favorite Places and Keywords*. AOL's keywords and Favorite
  Places won't call up another browser.

- *AOL Weblinks*. Double-clicking some forums on AOL brings up
  its Web browser. This capability doesn't function with a separate
  browser.

- *Newsgroups*. AOL uses a proprietary system for its newsgroup
  feature. Another news reading program won't work as part of the
  AOL connection (though this could change in the future).

- *Email*. AOL's email system is also proprietary and doesn't usually work with other email programs. But this situation will
  change. Upcoming versions of Microsoft's Outlook Express and
  Qualcomm's Eudora are expected to be designed to retrieve your
  AOL email.

Another Way to Get AOL Email   AOL has created a special program, NetMail, which is designed to let you access your AOL email if you connect to AOL via an Internet provider. It uses Microsoft Internet Explorer. To learn how to use this feature, just use the keyword **NetMail.**

USING INTERNET CHAT SOFTWARE

In Lesson 11, "Joining and Participating in an AOL Chat," I described how AOL's chats and online conferences work. Those features, of course, are restricted to AOL. In the next few pages, I tell you how to join an Internet chat on AOL.

A popular method of chatting on the Internet is called the Internet Relay Chat (or IRC for short). It's more involved than the chats on AOL. Here's how they differ:

- You can "talk" online with people across the world with Internet access, whether they are on AOL or not.

- You can join several chats at once. On AOL, you can only partic- ipate in a single chat or conference at any one time.

- IRC can be silly or outrageous or profane. AOL's Terms of Service don't apply when you go beyond the service, so it's very possible you may find some Internet chats to be offensive, and you should definitely consider not allowing your kids to join them.

FIRST THE SOFTWARE

In order to access an IRC, you need a special program, called an IRC client. AOL's software libraries have a number of these programs, some simple, some highly sophisticated. To check what's available, use the key- word **Internet** to access AOL's Internet Connection. Then click the Internet Extras button and then the Internet Software button (which brings up a listing such as the one shown in Figure 14.2).

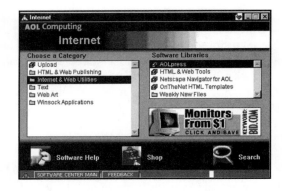

FIGURE 14.2   Here's a library of Internet software from AOL.

SETTING UP AN IRC CLIENT PROGRAM

To give you an idea of how IRC programs work, I've selected a popular shareware product, *mIRC*, written by Khaled Mardam-Bey (it's available in AOL's libraries). It's not your only choice, but it has the benefit of being relatively easy to install and set up, so you might want to give it a try (the author asks for $20 if you like it and want to continue to use it).

Here's how to install and configure mIRC. You can use this information as a guide in setting up other IRC software:

1. Download the software to your PC's drive. You'll find more information on locating and downloading software in Lesson 16, "Finding and Downloading Software from AOL."

2. Click your Windows 95 Start menu and choose Run.

3. Enter the full path and name of the file in the Run text field. In a typical example it would be C:\America Online 4.0\download\mirc511t.exe.

   You can also use the Browse feature in your Run window to help locate the file for you.

4. Press Enter and read the onscreen instructions.

5. Install the software.

USING YOUR NEW IRC SOFTWARE

When you first open an IRC program, you need to make a few settings so it can access chats as part of your AOL connection. A typical Setup screen (in this case for mIRC) is shown in Figure 14.3.

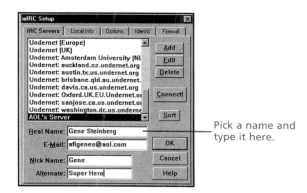

Pick a name and type it here.

FIGURE 14.3   Use this Setup window to enter your network and nickname preferences.

Here's what to do next:

1. Type your Real Name in the appropriate box.

2. Type your AOL Internet email address where requested. This is your AOL screen name followed by *@aol.com*. For example, my Internet address is aflgenes@aol.com.

3. Enter a nickname where requested. This nickname doesn't have to be your screen name or real name. It can be something else entirely. Don't be afraid to be imaginative in selecting it.

From here you need to select AOL's server as the place where the connections are made:

1. Click the Add button, which brings up the Add Server dialog box.

2. Name your new IRC server in the first list field. You can name it simply America Online.

3. Type **irc01.irc.aol.com** in the next list field.

4. If it's not already included, add **6667** as your Port #.

5. Add **Undernet** as the Group. Figure 14.4 shows how the entries appear on the setup screen.

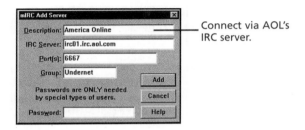

Connect via AOL's IRC server.

FIGURE **14.4**   Place your AOL network settings on this setup screen.

6. Click the Add button to include your network setting in the ARC servers listing. This step brings you back to the main Setup screen.

If the First Setting Doesn't Work...   If the AOL IRC server setting I suggested doesn't work for you, here's another one to try: Type **irc02.irc.aol.com** in the Enter Server field of the Add Server window. Use the same port setting **(6667)** and enter **EFnet** as the group.

THE NEXT STEP...

To log on to AOL's IRC server, select it in the list field, and then click the Connect! button. Within a few seconds, you see a window with the MODT!—that's the Message of the Day—from AOL and then the program's default mIRC Channels Folder (see Figure 14.5).

You can begin
Internet chats with
these sessions.

FIGURE 14.5   AOL includes a few channels for you to get your feet
wet.

To enter a chat, select the name by clicking it, and then click the Join
button. This opens your first IRC chat window (see Figure 14.6).

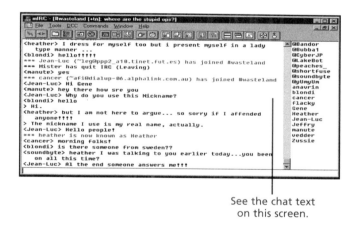

See the chat text
on this screen.

FIGURE 14.6   Here's an active chat already in progress.

If you've used AOL's own chat feature, you'll find that the IRC chat
screen has similar features. Enter your comment in the text field at the
bottom, and press the Return or Enter key to send it to the chat room.

Is Performance Slow? Sometimes AOL's own network traffic is heavy, especially during the evening "prime time" hours, and this can slow down performance. But Internet traffic is just plain unpredictable, and the two may slow your chat to a crawl at times. So just be patient or try again another time.

 Don't be Upset if They Eject You Each IRC is run by a "channel operator." They can be friendly or arbitrary, or both. And if you don't participate in a chat, they might just bump you (remove you from the chat). Or they might just do it for no reason because they want to, so don't be offended.

FINDING OTHER INTERNET CHATS

If you want to locate other active chats, click the List Channels icon in mIRC's program toolbar (it's sixth from the left in the version I examined).

You can use this feature to check for chats by topic, so you'll see only the ones listed that might interest you. When you've located an interesting chat, click the Join button to open it.

In this lesson, you learned how to use other Internet programs (including Internet Relay Chat software) with your AOL software.

LESSON 15

SETTING UP AUTOMATIC AOL SESSIONS

In this lesson you learn how to run your AOL sessions automatically, at the times you specify.

USING AUTOMATIC AOL

Normally, you log on to AOL when you want, check your email, look for messages, check forums and so forth, and then log off.

AOL has a special feature where you can do much of this online searching automatically. And you don't have to be seated in front of your computer to do it. Instead, you can use the Automatic AOL feature.

Before running an Automatic AOL session, you have to set it up. The first step is to select the Mail Center toolbar icon, choose Setup Automatic AOL from the drop-down menu, and then select the Walk Me Through icon. A screen similar to that in Figure 15.1 appears. AOL also sometimes refers to this feature as a FlashSession.

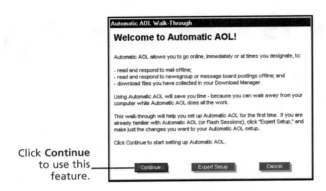

Click **Continue** to use this feature.

FIGURE 15.1 The walk-through feature makes it easy for you to set up your Automatic AOL sessions.

There's an Expert Setup Too! If you'd rather do all the setups at once, you can click the Expert Setup option, which is available by clicking the button on the first Walk-Through setup window.

AUTOMATIC EMAIL

To proceed with the Automatic AOL Walk-Through, click the Continue button. This brings up the screen shown in Figure 15.2 This screen gives you the option of getting your unread email during your Automatic AOL sessions.

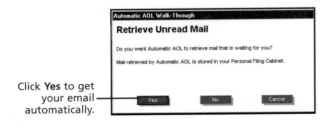

Click **Yes** to get your email automatically.

FIGURE 15.2 Do you want to access email during the automatic session?

If you decide to receive incoming email, you see the screen shown in Figure 15.3. The choice you have here is whether to download files attached to your email. Since there's no way to control whether to download or not, you may just want to turn off this option (you can always download the file later while online, after reading the message it came with).

Click **No** if you decide not to receive such file transfers (this choice is recommended).

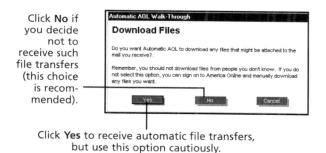

Click **Yes** to receive automatic file transfers, but use this option cautiously.

FIGURE **15.3**   This screen lets you choose whether to automatically download files attached to your email.

If you click the No option, you can still retrieve a file attachment for up to seven days after the mail is read.

The next choice to make during Walk-Through is whether to send your outgoing email automatically (see Figure 15.4). You can write all of your email offline, or you can write the email while still online, and then click the Send Later icon to have it mailed in a later Automatic AOL session.

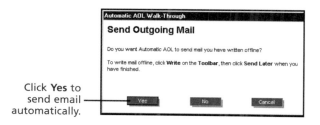

Click **Yes** to send email automatically.

FIGURE **15.4**   You can send your email automatically if you OK this option.

AUTOMATIC FILE TRANSFERS

In the choice shown in Figure 15.5, you can decide whether files marked for later downloading will be retrieved during the Automatic AOL session. I explain how to set up files in this fashion, by using AOL's Download Manager, in Lesson 16, "Finding and Downloading Software from AOL."

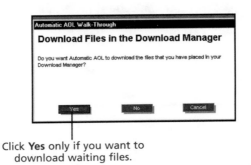

Click **Yes** only if you want to download waiting files.

FIGURE 15.5   Here you decide whether to retrieve files marked for later downloading.

AUTOMATIC MESSAGE BOARD VISITS

Automatic AOL can also be used to send and receive messages from both AOL's message boards and your Internet newsgroups. Before you can use this feature, though, you must mark the messages for offline reading (also see Lessons 10, "Using AOL Message Boards," and 12, "Visiting the Internet on AOL"). After you've chosen message boards to read offline, you can use the next screens to have them retrieved automatically.

PASSWORD SETTINGS

In order to log on to AOL automatically, you need to store your password in your AOL software (the screen is shown in Figure 15.6).

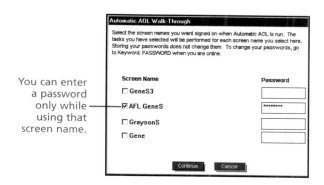

You can enter
a password
only while ———
using that
screen name.

FIGURE 15.6   Enter your password in this screen.

Be Cautious with Your Password   Remember that anyone who can access your computer can also use your AOL account if you store your password. So consider carefully whether to store your password in the program or not. You may also want to consider using a security program to prevent unauthorized access to your computer.

SCHEDULING THE SESSIONS

There are two ways to run your sessions. The first is "on demand," simply by clicking the Mail Center toolbar icon and selecting Activate Automatic AOL from the drop-down menu. When you choose Begin, the session starts right away.

But the beauty of an Automatic AOL session is the ability to run your sessions at the times you schedule, whether you're in front of your computer or not. The next screen in the Walk-Through process is used to set up the sessions (see Figure 15.7).

You can click **Cancel** at any time to stop the setup process.

FIGURE **15.7**   Click the Yes button if you want to automate your sessions, No if you don't.

Here's how to schedule the actual sessions:

1. Pick the days of the week when you wish to run your sessions.

2. Select how often to run your sessions (see Figure 15.8).

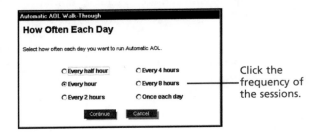

Click the frequency of the sessions.

FIGURE **15.8**   Click the box indicating how often your sessions are run.

3. Choose when to start your session.

After you've completed the Walk-Through, your Automatic AOL sessions will be set up. Just remember to keep your computer running during the scheduled time, so you won't miss a session. And of course you can't be connected to another service when your Automatic AOL session is supposed to occur.

WHERE'S THE EMAIL STORED?

The email you write to send during an Automatic AOL session is stored in a little file on your PC called the Personal Filing Cabinet. (You can check the stored email at anytime by using the Read Incoming/Saved Mail command in the Mail Center toolbar icon's drop-down menu.) You can check your email before it's sent, and delete it if you don't want it sent. After the email is sent, the messages are moved to the Mail You've Sent folder.

In this lesson, you discovered how Automatic AOL is a convenient way to send and retrieve email and message board posts at the times you select.

LESSON 16

FINDING AND DOWNLOADING SOFTWARE FROM AOL

In this lesson you learn how easy it is to locate and download software from AOL.

AOL'S SOFTWARE LIBRARIES OFTEN COME FIRST

AOL has literally tens of thousands of files in its software libraries. You can select from such items as arcade games, reminder programs, or an update to one of your own programs.

 Downloading   Receiving a file from its source (in this case AOL's host computer) to your PC.

 Uploading   Sending a file from your PC direct to another location, such as AOL.

USING VIRUS PROTECTION SOFTWARE

AOL's community leaders (the people who run the forums) check all files they post for known computer viruses. But you should still get the latest virus protection software yourself, as protection against newer viruses.

Virus software is especially important if you download files from Internet sources, which may or may not be checked before being made available. You can get more information about computer viruses from AOL's Virus Information Center, at keyword **Virus**.

 Look Before You Download! It's a sad fact that some people send virus-infected files via email as a prank. You should *never* download a file from someone you don't know. For more information about dealing with this sort of situation, use the keyword **Notify AOL**.

FINDING THE FILES YOU WANT

AOL's software libraries are searchable, so you don't have to guess where a file can be found. Here's how to use the file search feature:

1. Press **Ctrl+K** to bring up AOL's keyword window.

2. The keyword **File Search** to bring up the search window.

3. Click the Shareware icon to produce the search screen shown in Figure 16.1.

   As you see in Figure 16.1, you can search by category, by clicking the appropriate topic, or by timeframe.

Enter your search request in the text field.

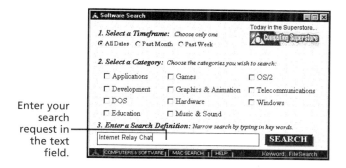

FIGURE 16.1 It's easy to search for software in AOL's libraries.

4. To start your search, enter the software's name or category in the search definition field.

5. Click Search.

   You'll see a screen message if the files you want to locate can't be found.

6. If files are found, a File Search Results window appears onscreen (see Figure 16.2).

Double-click the file-
name to learn more.

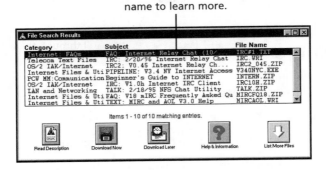

FIGURE 16.2   Here's a list of files that meet the description you gave.

7. Double-click a file's name or choose the Read Description button to learn more about a file (see Figure 16.3).

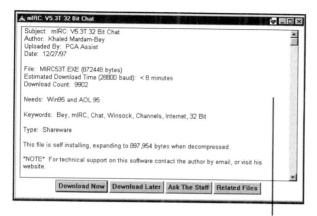

Scroll through the text
window to see all of it.

FIGURE 16.3   This is the description of a typical AOL file.

HOW TO DOWNLOAD FILES

There are two ways to download files:

- *Download Now.* Choose this option to transfer the file to your computer right away.

- *Download Later.* This option puts the file in a waiting queue, and it adds it to your Download Manager. You can consult the Download Manager at any time, by selecting it from the My Files toolbar icon's drop-down menu.

To start the download process:

1. Click Download Now, which brings up a window where you are asked to specify where your file is to be sent (see Figure 16.4).

2. If you want, rename the file (this isn't really necessary).

3. Click the Save button or press the Return or Enter key to begin downloading.

Click **Save** to
start the file
transfer.

FIGURE 16.4   Where do you wish to save your file?

    Prime Time on AOL Is Slower!   AOL usually runs
slower during prime time evening hours. It's usually
best to download in the early morning or middle of
the day (except for weekends, when it can be busy
throughout the day).

The file transfer's progress is shown by a progress bar, as shown
in Figure 16.5.

Click **Finish**
Later if you
wish to
resume the
download
later on.

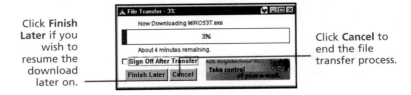

Click **Cancel** to
end the file
transfer process.

FIGURE 16.5   The download time is estimated by AOL.

When the download is done, AOL's narrator will announce "File's done!"

USING THE DOWNLOAD LATER OPTION

The Download Later option adds the file to a queue, which you can consult by opening the Download Manager from the My Files toolbar's drop-
down menu. See Figure 16.6 for a typical list of waiting files.

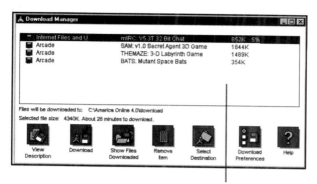

Double-click a filename (while
online) to get its description.

FIGURE 16.6   Here's the list of files waiting to be download.

Here are the features available to you in AOL's Download Manager (you
have to be online for most of them):

- *View Description.* Use this feature to double-check whether you
  still want the file or just want to learn more about it (but you
  must be online to see it).

- *Download.* Start downloading the files you've selected.

- *Show Files Downloaded.* Check a listing of the files recently
  transferred to your PC.

- *Remove Item.* Remove the selected item from the Download
  Manager's list.

- *Select Destination.* Pick the directory to which you want to
  transfer the files (by default is C:/America Online 4.0
  /download).

- *Download Preferences.* Set preferences for downloading here.

- *Help.* Get online assistance if you encounter a problem.

Print the File Description   The file description often includes basic installation instructions for the software you're downloading. It's a good idea to print a copy, by using the Print command from the File menu.

HOW TO USE THE FILES YOU'VE DOWNLOADED

Larger files on AOL are compressed, a process that uses special software to make the file smaller (and reduces the time it takes to transfer to your PC).

By default, your AOL software will automatically expand (restore) the file to its original state when you log off (this is a Download Manager preference you can change if you wish).

When you pick a file to download, check the file description to be sure you can run it. For example, if you have a PC with a 486 processor, don't bother with files that require a Pentium (or vice versa).

Sometimes, when you try to open a file, you may see a message that it's been damaged (or it simply won't run as it's supposed to do). If this happens, just delete the file and download it again. Sometimes noise on the phone line or an AOL network problem will cause a file to be damaged when it's sent to you.

RESUMING FILE DOWNLOADS

On occasion, a file download will end through no fault of your own. Your connection to AOL may end or AOL's host computer may have a problem.

If this occurs, *don't move or delete the partial file that's already been downloaded.* When you get back online, choose Download Manager from the My Files icon's drop-down menu, select the file, and then select the file from the listing and click the Download button to resume the file transfer.

FINDING THE FILE

When your file download is started, you normally select the target location (the default, as I've said, is the C:\America Online 4.0\download directory). You can switch this to another location if you prefer. If you find the file doesn't seem to be there, just bring up Windows Explorer to find it. Because the filename isn't always obvious, you may want to double-check the Download Manager list first.

WHAT KIND OF SOFTWARE IS THERE ON AOL?

Here are the types of software available:

- *Commercial software*. This is a retail product, available from your local computer store, mail-order dealer, or even one of AOL's online merchants. Sometimes commercial software comes in an "unboxed" version. You download a copy from AOL, and then send the merchant your payment information (it usually has to be done via credit card), and he will give you the password you need to open the file and use it.

- *Demoware*. This software is designed to showcase a product. You can try some or all of the features, but they won't work completely. For example, printing may be disabled, or there will be a time limit on use (a week or two mostly). If you like the product, you pay for it, and the publisher will give you the password to make the software completely functional.

- *Shareware*. The modern equivalent of the honor system. The author or publisher lets you use the software, usually with all features intact. If you like it, you are expected to pay its price within 15 to 30 days or so. Sometimes shareware will come with a reminder to send the money, which is usually a lot less than an equivalent commercial product. But don't attach price to value. Shareware is often written by some very smart programmers and it can be a better value than a commercial product. If you continue to use shareware, please pay the author or publisher, so it will continue to be developed and supported.

- *Freeware*. As the name implies, the software is free, but the author or publisher retains rights to the program. You'll find lots of useful utilities in this category in AOL's libraries.

- *Public Domain*. Such software can be used and distributed freely. The author or publisher doesn't have any rights to the program.

Finding the Latest Software Releases!   Use the keyword **Hot Software** to see the latest offerings from AOL's Computing channel.

Have Software of Interest to Others?   If you're a budding software author or you have a file you'd like to share with other members, consider uploading it. AOL's libraries will usually have an Upload area where you can send a file. But remember, you should not try to upload a file unless you have the right to do so. A commercial software update, for example, usually can be sent only by the publisher.

In this lesson, you learned how to find files on AOL and how to transfer them to your PC.

LESSON 17

USING AOL'S MEMBER HELP FORUMS

In this lesson you learn about AOL's online help system.

USING THE MEMBER HELP FORUMS

If you have a problem with your AOL software that's not discussed here, you can consult the Help menu. To access it, simply open Help from the menu bar, which brings up the screen shown in Figure 17.1.

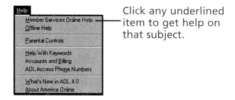

Click any underlined item to get help on that subject.

FIGURE **17.1** Choose the Help category for more information.

Print Your Help Text To print your help text, simply choose Print from the File menu.

VISITING THE MEMBER SERVICE AREA

If the Help menu doesn't answer your question, or you want to check your current AOL bill, simply visit the Member Services area (shown in Figure 17.2). You can get there by choosing Member Services from the Help menu or by the keyword **Help**.

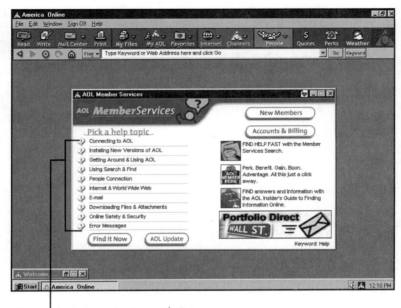

Choose the help topics from this list.

FIGURE 17.2   Visit AOL's Member Services area for more assistance.

AOL's DOWNLOAD HELP CENTER

If you run into problems downloading files, or just have some additional questions, you can access AOL's download help area. Just follow these steps:

1. Choose Member Services from the Help menu.

2. Double-click Downloading Files & Attachments from the topic list, which brings up the screen shown in Figure 17.3.

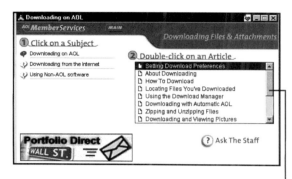

Double-click a topic for
more information.

FIGURE 17.3   Here's where you can get file download assistance
from AOL.

In addition to assistance with downloads, AOL's Member Services area
also provides help with email, Internet access, setting up your modem,
and more. If you cannot find a topic that suits, click the Find It Now button, at the bottom left in the forum screen shown in Figure 17.2, and enter
the topic description.

GETTING HELP FROM OTHER MEMBERS

Keyword: **MHM**

You'll find your fellow AOL members are often ready and willing to
assist. In fact, AOL's Members Helping Members forum (see Figure 17.4)
is designed with that purpose in mind. Here you can ask questions and get
answers from knowledgeable online visitors. And as you become more
familiar with the ins and outs of AOL, you may decide to contribute information there too.

Get help from other AOL
members in this forum.

FIGURE 17.4   AOL members participate in the Members Helping
Members forum.

A Source for Help with New AOL Software   When
new AOL software comes out, a special forum is there
to assist with information about the new features and
how to deal with problems. You can find the forum at
the keyword **Upgrade**.

What's Your AOL Bill Look Like?   If you have a question about your AOL bill, or you wish to change the
billing arrangement, use the keyword **Billing** and follow the screens to get the information you need.

GETTING INTERACTIVE SUPPORT FROM AOL

If text files and message boards won't solve your problem, there's another
way. It's called Member Help Interactive (sometimes called Tech Live),
and it consists of chat rooms staffed by AOL representatives.

Because Member Help Interactive is designed as a "last resort" for members, getting there can sometimes be a little tricky. Here's how to do it:

1. Open any Member Services Help topic (see Figure 17.5).

Pick your help topic
from this screen.

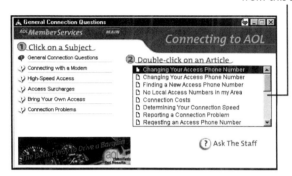

FIGURE **17.5**   This is your first step on the road to getting interactive help from AOL.

2. Click the Ask The Staff button, which brings up information on how to get further assistance.

3. Choose option three, which includes a direct link to AOL's Tech Live Auditorium. When you click that link you see the screen shown in Figure 17.6.

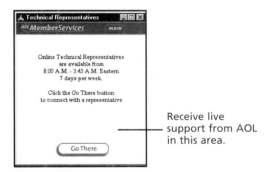

Receive live
support from AOL
in this area.

FIGURE **17.6**   Here's where AOL representatives can help you on a one-on-one basis. The hours shown here may change.

A Cool Way To Save Money on AOL!   If you are already a member of an Internet provider, such as AT&T WorldNet, EarthLink or Netcom, you can save money on your AOL bill. Just call up AOL's Billing center (at keyword **Billing**) and sign up for the "Bring Your Own Access" plan.

In this lesson you learned how to use AOL's online help system. You'll also want to read Lesson 18, "Common Solutions to Common Problems," for tips and tricks on solving common AOL problems.

LESSON 18

COMMON SOLUTIONS TO COMMON PROBLEMS

In this lesson you learn about timesaving tips and tricks to help you get over the rough spots if you have a problem on AOL.

GETTING OVER THE ROUGH SPOTS

It's a sure thing that sometimes things just won't work properly during your AOL sessions (nothing is ever perfect in PC-land). But there are usually simple solutions. In the following pages I'm going to cover some of the most common questions along with the answers.

OLD VERSION STILL INSTALLED?

Question: Okay, I've downloaded the newest AOL software, but I don't see a difference. What's wrong?

Answer: In order to use the new software, it has to be installed. Fortunately, most new AOL installers these days will start the installation automatically once you log off. So watch for that. If it doesn't happen, check the installer file and run it manually.

MESS UP YOUR TOOLBAR?

Question: I tried to customize AOL's toolbar by dragging some Favorite Places icons to it. But now it's too large, and I want to change it back. How do I do that?

Answer: Just hold down the Ctrl key and drag the icons, one at a time, from the toolbar. If the toolbar looks too wide to you, you can remove the Stock Quotes, Perks, and Weather icons too, in the same fashion.

DO YOU USE A MACINTOSH TOO?

Question: We have an Apple Macintosh computer at the office. I'd like to be able to check my AOL account there, too. Is it possible?

Answer: Yes, it is. There is also a version of AOL's software available to Macintosh users. And it looks and works very much the same as the Windows version you're using. If you have an AOL CD-ROM, you'll probably find a Macintosh version on there too (but it'll only be accessible when you load the CD-ROM on a Macintosh).

SOLUTIONS TO COMMON MODEM PROBLEMS

Question: The noise my modem is making is disturbing. Is there any way to make it lower or turn it off?

Answer: Yes, but you have to do an Expert Setup and fix the modem strings.

Here's how:

1. Open your AOL software, but don't log on.

2. Click the Setup button.

3. Choose Expert Setup from the next screen.

4. On the next screen, click the Devices (modems, and so on) tab.

5. Select your modem's name, and then click the Edit button at the bottom right of the screen.

6. On the next screen, labeled Expert Edit Modem, click the Edit Commands button, which brings up the screen in Figure 18.1.

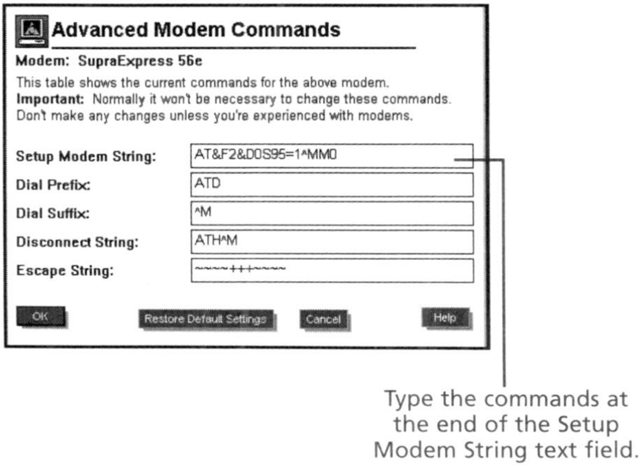

Advanced Modem Commands

Modem: SupraExpress 56e

This table shows the current commands for the above modem.
Important: Normally it won't be necessary to change these commands.
Don't make any changes unless you're experienced with modems.

Setup Modem String:	AT&F2&D0S95=1^MM0
Dial Prefix:	ATD
Dial Suffix:	^M
Disconnect String:	ATH^M
Escape String:	~~~+++~~~

OK   Restore Default Settings   Cancel   Help

Type the commands at
the end of the Setup
Modem String text field.

FIGURE 18.1   Create your custom modem settings here.

1. Type **M0** (that's a zero, folks!) at the end of the Setup Modem String text field. Don't enter it between any other command or change anything else!

2. Click OK on this screen, OK or Close the other setup screens, to activate your changes.

The M0 command will silence most modems. If you just want to make it lower, insert the command **L1** instead. On some modems, such as the U.S. Robotics Courier V. Everything, the command won't work, because the modem itself has a volume control to adjust the level.

Question: I just installed my new 56K modem, but it's still connecting at 2400bps. What's wrong?

Answer: In order to connect at the highest possible speed, you need to use an AOL access number that supports the speed. To check for access numbers in your city, choose AOL Access Phone Numbers from the Help menu. Then enter the area code of the city for which you want a number. Each listed phone number will include its maximum potential connection speed.

Question: I'm being disconnected all the time from AOL. Why can't they fix this?

Answer: It's not always AOL's fault. Here are some reasons for such problems:

- *Noisy phone line.* First try another access number, but, if the problem still occurs (and maybe you hear static on the line), call the phone company.

- *Too many phones.* Each phone device you add to your line (including answering machines, fax machines, and more phones) uses electrical current from the phone line. If you have too many devices, it may hurt the quality of the modem's connection. A quick way to check this is to remove some other devices and see if things improve.

- *Signals from call waiting.* If you're using call waiting, be sure it's disabled (if that's possible) by using the appropriate check box in your AOL Connection Locations setup box. Otherwise, the beep that sounds when another call is coming through can disconnect you from AOL.

Question: Now, suddenly, I can't connect to AOL anymore. It just won't dial out. Help!

Answer: Have you changed your computer setup? That could be a reason. Here are some things to check:

- *Modem hangs up.* Sometimes a modem can freeze up, just like your PC. If it's an external modem, turn it off and on again. If it's an internal modem, restart Windows.

- *Try other software.* Try your ISP connection or HyperTerminal and see if the modem dials out.

- *Check the prefix.* Maybe you need a special number to dial out. A business or hotel may require a special number to make an outside call (such as an "8" or a "9"). This can be fixed simply by opening AOL's Setup box, choosing Expert Setup, and double-clicking the phone number you are using. It will bring up a dialog box where you can enter the dial prefix.

IS AOL OFF THE AIR?

Question: I'm positive all my settings are correct, but I still can't connect to AOL. It stops at step 6, or when checking my password. What's wrong?

Answer: From time to time AOL shuts down the service for maintenance. Sometimes you'll see a screen to the effect that the service is unavailable with an estimate of when it will be working again. But sometimes you don't. For up-to-date listings of AOL maintenance, use the keyword **AOL Insider.**

WHERE'S MY SOUND?

Question: Suddenly my sounds are gone. When I log on to AOL, there's no "Welcome" sound, and there's no sound when email arrives. How do I fix this?

Answer: The first thing to do is check to make sure your Windows sounds (such as the sound you hear when Windows has opened on your PC) are working. If not, check your sound card and drivers to be sure they're set up properly. If your Windows sounds work properly, open your Sounds Control Panel and look for AOL's sounds from the scrolling list. You may have to relink (associate) these sounds to get them to function. This problem may happen, sometimes, when you upgrade to an all-new version of AOL's software.

WHY'S THE REQUEST TAKING SO LONG?

Question: When I try to bring up my email or go to a forum, I get a message that the host has taken too long. What host? What's wrong?

Answer: Your modem and AOL's host computer are constantly communicating back and forth. You ask to visit a forum, and AOL has to deliver the information to your modem. If the communication breaks down because of a connection or network problem, you'll get that message about the problem with the host. Usually, if you log off AOL and log on again, the problem will be gone. If the problem continues, switch to another AOL connection number, if available, or just try again at a different hour. For more information on dealing with this problem, use the keyword **System Response**.

WHY DO THEY WANT MY PASSWORD?

Question: Help! I keep getting Instant Messages or email from people who tell me my account is messed up and they need my password or credit card information. What should I tell them?

Answer: Nothing! *Don't respond to those messages!* Remember, as the email and Instant Message screens on AOL state, *nobody from AOL will ever ask you online for your password or credit card information!* There are folks who send out those fake messages hoping a member might give them the information, so they can steal your account or password. When you get these fake requests, use the keyword **Notify AOL** to report the offender. AOL will take care of the rest.

MY MESSAGE BOARD POST DISAPPEARED

Question: I posted a message and checked it. Now it's not there. Why did they remove it?

Answer: Maybe AOL didn't remove it. When you read a message, it is marked as read, and so it doesn't show up the next time you check for it. To see all the recent messages (even the ones you've already read) use the Find Since feature on a message board. But it is also true that AOL's community leaders may sometimes remove a message because you posted it in the wrong place, posted it over and over again, or they don't think the language is appropriate. Please read Lesson 10, "Using AOL Message Boards," for advice on how to use AOL's message boards.

UNSOLICITED EMAIL

Question: I'm getting tons and tons of messages advertising work-at-home plans, erotic Web sites, and other stuff I'm not interested in. How do I stop them?

Answer: Because AOL is the world's largest online service, it's a target for promotions. And, like the junk mail you get in your regular mail box, you will often get unsolicited offers while online. One way to control this is to use AOL's Mail Controls feature. You just have to connect to AOL using your master screen name (the first one in the drop-down list of screen names), and use the keyword **Mail Controls** to access the feature. There you can select locations from which you don't want to receive mail. If you still receive such offers, forward the message to the screen name **TOSEmail1** and AOL will investigate the matter. See Lesson 19, "AOL's Neighborhood Watch," for more information on customizing your AOL experience (especially if your children are using the service).

WHERE DID THAT WEB SITE GO?

Question: I've tried and tried to reach my favorite Web site, and now it's gone. I get a message that the URL can't be found. What am I doing wrong?

Answer: The first thing to do is make sure the URL is typed exactly. If you type even a single letter or number wrong, it won't work. And sometimes a Web site may be off the air, or the URL has changed. If the problem continues to occur, use AOL's NetFind feature to check to see if there's a new address for the site.

WHY'S MY WEB PERFORMANCE SO SLOW?

Question: Whenever I try to connect to a Web site, the process seems to just take forever. What can I do?

Answer: Sometimes it's the fault of AOL's host computer. But it may be a problem with the Web site itself. Usually, those sites are run by a single computer, and if lots of folks like you are trying to access it, performance may bog down. Another way to help speed up Web access is to make sure you have a good connection to AOL. Sometimes logging off and logging on again may help. It's also true that the Web requires a modem of at least 14,400bps capability (and higher). If you have a slow modem, it may be time to upgrade.

CAN'T CONNECT VIA FTP?

Question: I keep trying to get to an FTP site, but I always see a message that there are too many users. What do I do?

Answer: Just try again later. Many of these sites are run by personal computers, possibly similar to the one you have. They can only handle a small number of users at any one time, and if more people try to get to the site, you see a message that it's not available.

SYSTEM CRASHING?

Question: I keep getting crashes while I'm connected to AOL. Why can't they make this software work properly?

Answer: Software isn't perfect, and sometimes it'll crash (and often for no obvious reason). Here are some things to consider:

- If you're running other programs, exit them, restart Windows, and see if AOL works okay. Maybe the problem is due to the interaction of other software.

- If you got your new AOL software as a result of a public preview, use the keyword **Preview** again to check to see if a newer version is available. Preview means the program is not quite in release form yet, and AOL is just letting members use it to help fix the remaining problems (and, of course, create demand for the new software). A preview can sometimes continue for a few months before the final release is out.

- Reinstall your AOL software. A system crash can also damage a file needed by your software. When you reinstall, the files are replaced. When you install the software, you have the option to overwrite the previous version, or install in a new directory. It may be better to try installing in a new directory and see if the new version works properly.

- If the problems continue, contact AOL customer service for assistance. It may be necessary for some back-and-forth communication to figure out the source of the problem.

In this lesson you learned easy solutions to deal with common problems you might confront on AOL or with your AOL software.

LESSON 19

AOL's NEIGHBORHOOD WATCH

In this lesson you learn about AOL's Neighborhood Watch and how to provide the safest possible online experience for your kids.

AOL IS USUALLY FRIENDLY, BUT...

One of the reasons AOL became number one is because it's advertised as family-safe. Another, of course, is its clever marketing of the service.

However, as in any large city, some of the folks online are not quite so friendly, and they don't have your child's best interests in mind.

Here are some things to look out for:

- *Inappropriate material.* AOL doesn't allow vulgar or sexually explicit material online. But that doesn't stop people from ignoring the rules.

- *Face-to-face meetings.* Don't allow your child to have a personal meeting with anyone he met on AOL unless you're around to monitor the situation. In any case, it's never a good idea to give out your own address. Meetings are best held in a public place.

- *Online harassment.* Don't sit still if your child gets offensive email or Instant Messages. Report the problem via keyword **Notify AOL.**

- *Internet Access.* The Internet is the wild, wild west compared to AOL. It is largely uncontrolled in terms of checking for acceptable content. A little later in this lesson I tell you how to set up AOL's Parental Controls feature to customize your child's access to the Internet.

VISITING NEIGHBORHOOD WATCH

Keyword: **Neighborhood Watch**

AOL has set up a special area where parents can get assistance in dealing with online problems and in protecting our children. It's called Neighborhood Watch (see Figure 19.1).

Information about AOL's online safety features

Set Parental Controls.

Learn how to stop junk email.

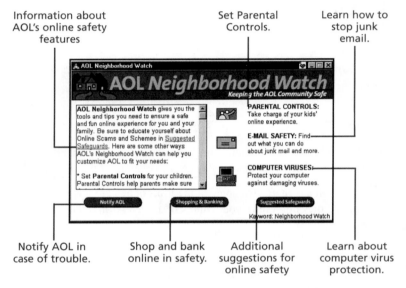

Notify AOL in case of trouble.

Shop and bank online in safety.

Additional suggestions for online safety

Learn about computer virus protection.

FIGURE **19.1**   This area is designed to help provide a safer online experience.

Your Kids Should Get Their Own Screen Names!   The only way to give your children a custom experience is to give them their own screen name. You can have up to five names on your account (including the one you first created when you joined AOL). Use the keyword **Names** to create more screen names.

USING PARENTAL CONTROLS

Keyword: **Parental Controls**

With AOL's Parental Controls feature (see Figure 19.2), you can customize the online experience for anyone using your account. To use this feature, you need to log on using your master screen name (the one at the top of the drop-down list of names).

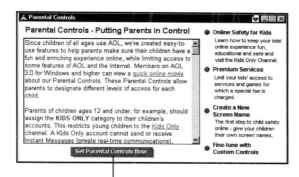

After reading the information here,
click Set Parental Controls Now.

FIGURE **19.2**   Provide a safer online environment with Parental Controls.

To start using this feature, click Set Parental Controls Now, which produces the setup screen shown in Figure 19.3.

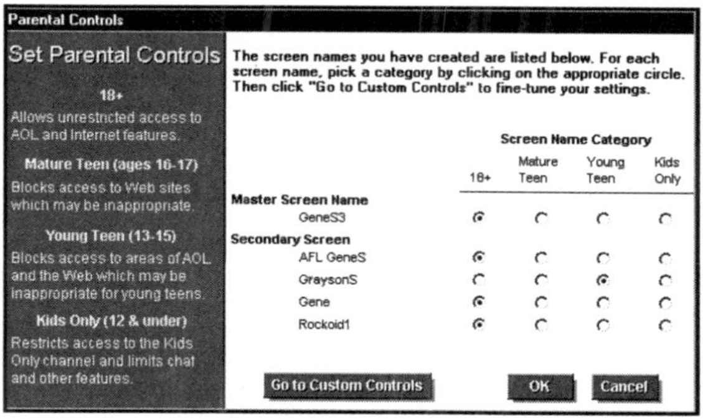

FIGURE **19.3**   Use this dialog box to set up Parental Controls.

AOL has some preconfigured settings you might want to try:

- *18+*. This is the standard setting. It gives you full access to all regular AOL and Internet-based features.

- *Mature Teen*. Designed for those from 16 to 17, this setting limits Internet access to specific sites approved by AOL.

- *Young Teen*. Designed for children ages 13 through 15. The major restriction is to Internet-based sites, and email attachments.

- *Kids Only*. This is the most restricted setting. It gives your children access strictly to the Kids Only channel, approved Web sites, and prevents receiving email with attached files.

SETTING CUSTOM PARENTAL CONTROLS

In addition to the standard settings, you can configure each setting separately to your taste. Simply use the Custom Controls options (as shown in Figure 19.4).

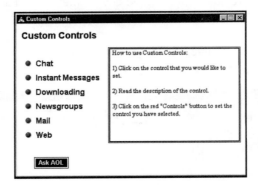

FIGURE 19.4   Six different access categories for AOL can be customized here.

Each element of your child's access can be customized by using the Custom Controls options (again see Figure 19.4). Custom settings can be made for Chat, Instant Messages, Downloading, Newsgroups Email, and the Web.

SETTING MAIL CONTROLS

Mass email is one common online problem. You get offers for work-at-home schemes, erotic material, discount computers, and so on. Some of these offers, of course, may be real. But most of it is unwelcome. AOL has gone to court to stop some of the firms who sent this email from flooding your mail box.

You can also take steps to control the email you or your children receive. To make these settings:

1. Click the button to the left of the Mail option in the Custom Controls screen shown earlier in Figure 19.4.

2. Click the Mail Controls button that appears at the bottom of the next screen to bring up the list of screen names.

3. Select the screen name for which you are making your settings.

4. Click Edit to bring up the setup panel shown in Figure 19.5.

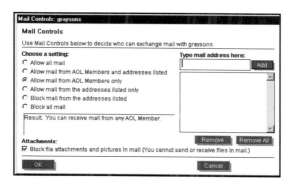

FIGURE 19.5   Use this feature to customize your AOL email settings.

5. Enter your email settings (you set them separately for each screen name on your account).

6. After the settings are completed, click OK to put them into effect.

AOL's Terms of Service

Keyword: **TOS**

When you join AOL, you agree to accept its Terms of Service, the rules governing use of the service. It's very possible you haven't read those terms, in the same fashion that you pass by a software license you see on the screen.

It's a good idea to check those terms (see Figure 19.6) because you may run into situations where you encounter online harassment or your children get a little mischievous and misbehave online.

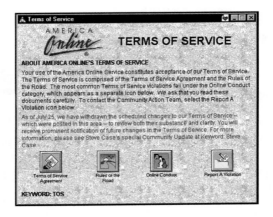

FIGURE 19.6   Examine AOL's Terms of Service here.

The Terms of Service consist to a great degree of common-sense issues. You are expected to refrain from using vulgar or abusive language, and you shouldn't harass or upset other members or disrupt an online conference. In addition, the exchange of nude or explicit material isn't allowed on AOL.

Reporting Problems

If someone annoys you online, or you see a violation, use the keyword **Notify AOL** (see Figure 19.7) to report the problem.

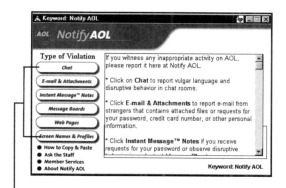

Click the item that applies
  to the online problem.

FIGURE **19.7**   Report Terms of Service problems on AOL here.

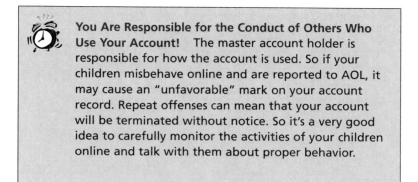

You Are Responsible for the Conduct of Others Who Use Your Account!   The master account holder is responsible for how the account is used. So if your children misbehave online and are reported to AOL, it may cause an "unfavorable" mark on your account record. Repeat offenses can mean that your account will be terminated without notice. So it's a very good idea to carefully monitor the activities of your children online and talk with them about proper behavior.

In this lesson you learned how to use AOL's Parental Controls and Mail Controls features to provide a safer online experience.

INDEX

SYMBOLS

56K modems, 2
800 phone numbers, 17
888 phone numbers, 17
28,000bps modems, 2

A

About this Forum icons on
  forums, 33
access numbers, 8
    finding new, 14-17
accessing AOL from
  Macintoshes, 156
account information
        keyword, Billing, 152
        rates for multiple providers, 113
Address Book, 77-78
addresses, email, 69-72
    see also screen names
advertising on forums,
  Classifieds, 48
AFK (Away From Keyboard)
  smiley, 105
answering email, 74-75
anti-virus software, 140-141
AOL
        accessing from
          Macintoshes, 156
        customizing toolbars, problems,
          155-156
        finding members, 86-87
        installing, problems with
          versions, 155
AOL Live conference room, 34,
  101-102
AOL Store keyword, 46
AOLpress, 115-116
art, *see* graphics

Ask-a-Teacher feature, 66-67
attaching files to email, 75-76
audio problems, 159
Automatic AOL sessions, 133-134
        email, 134-135, 139
        file transfers, 136
        message board visits, 136
        password settings, 136-137
        scheduling, 137-138
        Walk-Through
            email, 134-135
            scheduling sessions,
            137-138

B

BAK (Back At Keyboard)
  smiley, 105
Billing keyword, 34
BRB (Be Right Back) smiley, 105
Buddy List, 83-85
business information
        channels
            Personal Finance, 39-41
            Travel, 50-52
            WorkPlace, 36-37
        forums, tax, 42-44
        Internet commerce, PrimeHost,
          37-39
        Quotes and Portfolios center,
          41-42
        Web pages, 123

C

channels, 26-28
        Channels drop-down menu, 25
        Computing, latest available soft-
          ware, 148

Entertainment, 53-54
    Movies forum, 54-55
finding, Find Central, 28-32
forums, checking, 89
Games, 55-57
Influence, 63-64
News, 60-62
Personal Finance, 39-41
Research & Learn, 64-66
Shopping, 45-50
Sports, 57-59
subject-oriented newspapers
    and magazines, 63
Travel, 50-52
WorkPlace, 36-37
Chat protocol, 104
chat rooms, 99
    channels, 26
    custom settings for children,
        167
    entering, 99-101
    etiquette, 100, 104
    Member Help Interactive,
        152-154
    smileys, 104-105
children online
    custom settings, 167
    guidelines, 163
    Neighborhood Watch, 164
    Parental Controls, 165-167
    reporting irregularities, 168-169
    Terms of Service, 168
Classifieds forum, 48
clip art, Web pages, 119-120
color (type and background),
    formatting email, 69-70
commands, toolbar icons, 22-25
commercial software, 147
Community Action Team, reporting
    irregular requests, 50
conference rooms, 34, 99-102
    participating in, 102-103
    smileys/emoticons, 104-105
configuring
    AOL software, 18-19
    mIRC, 128
connections, local, 8
    finding additional access
        numbers, 14-17

Connectix Surf Express, 126
copies of email, 69
credit cards, ordering
    merchandise, 46

D

demoware, 147
downloading files
    AOL software types, 147-148
    custom settings for
        children, 167
    Download Help Center, 150-151
    Download Later option,
        144-146
    Download Now option,
        143-144
    finding downloads, 147
    from AOL software
        libraries, 140
    from Internet, 110
    from unknown sources,
        140-141
    resuming downloads, 146
    using downloaded files, 146
    see also transferring files

E

educational opportunities
    Ask-A-Teacher feature, 66-67
    Homework Help feature, 66-67
    Research & Learn channel,
        64-66
email
    Address Book, 77-78
    answering, 74-75
    Automatic AOL sessions,
        134-135, 139
    compared to message boards,
        88-89
    custom settings for
        children, 167
    formatting, 69-70
    graphics
        attaching, 75-76
        inserting, 71
    Instant Messages, 79-82
        Buddy List, 83-85
        similar conversations with
            Instant Messenger, 82-83

mailing lists, 112
receiving, 72-74
  News Profiles, 62
requests for passwords or credit
  card information, 160
saving, 76
security, downloading files, 76
sending
  AOL, 70-71
  Internet, 71-72
  with attached files, 75-76
unsolicited, 160-161
writing, 68-69
emoticons, 104-105
Entertainment channel, 53-54
  forums, Movies, 54-55
etiquette (online)
  chat rooms, 100-104
  message boards, 97

F

Fantasy Leagues, 58
Favorite Places message boards, 92
Favorites drop-down menu, 25
fee-based ads, 48
file transfer protocol, *see* FTP
files
  attaching to email, 75-76
  downloading
    AOL software types,
      147-148
    custom settings for
      children, 167
    Download Later option,
      144-146
    Download Now option,
      143-144
    finding downloads, 147
    resuming downloads, 146
    using downloaded
      files, 146
  finding with File Search,
    141-143
  transferring
    across Internet, 110
    Automatic AOL
      sessions, 136
    from unknown sources,
      140-141

Find Central, finding information or
  services, 28-32
finding
  downloaded files, 147
  information or services, Find
    Central, 28-32
  Internet information, Gopher
    and NetFind, 111
  software
    AOL software
      libraries, 140
    Download Help Center,
      150-151
    with File Search, 141-143
fonts, formatting email, 69-70
forums, 33
  Channels, 26
  Classifieds, 48
  Members Helping Members,
    151-152
  Movies, 54-55
  tax, 42-44
free ads, 48
freeware, 148
FTP (file transfer protocol),
  accessing sites, 162

G-H

GA (Go Ahead) smiley, 105
Games channel, 55-57
GlobalNet service, 17
GMTA (Great Minds Think Alike)
  smiley, 105
Gopher, 111
Grandstand keyword, 58
graphics
  email, 69-770
    attaching, 75-76
    inserting, 71
  Web pages
    backgrounds, 118-119
    clip art, 119-120

hardware requirements, AOL
  installation, 1-2
headlines, Web pages, 118
help
  chat rooms, Member Help
    Interactive, 152-154

Download Help Center,
    150-151
forums, Members Helping
    Members, 151-152
keyword, 34
Member Services, 149-150
menu, 149
home pages, 115-116
    Personal Publisher, 116-117
        background art, 118-119
        clip art, 119-120
        previewing, 121-122
        templates, 117-118
        text, 120-121
        titles/headlines, 118
        viewing, 122
Homework Help feature, 66-67

I

IHTBHWYG (It's Hard To Be
    Humble When You're Great)
    smiley, 105
IMO (In My Opinion) smiley, 105
Influence channel, 64
information, finding, Find Central,
    28-32
IMHO (In My Humble/Honest
    Opinion) smiley, 105
installing
    AOL, 1
        adding to Start menu, 5-6
        new or over existing
            versions, 4
        on Windows 3.x, 4
        on Windows 95 or 98, 3-4
        problems with
            versions, 155
        requirements, 2
    mIRC, 128
Instant Messages, 79-82
    Buddy List, 83-85
    custom settings for
        children, 167
    requests for passwords or credit
        card information, 160
    similar conversations with
        Instant Messenger, 82-83
Instant Messenger, 82-83

Internet
    commerce, PrimeHost, 37-39
    drop-down menu, 25
    email
        answering, 74-75
        receiving, 72-74
        sending, 71-72
    Instant Messenger, 82-83
    IRCs (Internet Relay
        Chats), 127
        client programs, 127-130
        finding active chats, 132
        logging on to AOL IRC
            server, 130-132
    services, 106-108
        AOL, connecting to, from
            other ISPs, 113-114
        FTP (file transfer
            protocol), 111
        Gopher, 111
        mailing lists, 112
        NetFind, 111
        Newsgroups, 109-110
        rates for multiple
            providers, 113
        Web browsers, 108
    see also Web sites
Internet Explorer, *see* Microsoft
    Internet Explorer
Internet service providers, *see* ISPs
Intuit tax forums, 42
IRCs (Internet Relay Chats), 127
    client programs, 127-130
    finding active chats, 132
    logging on to AOL server,
        130-132
ISPs (Internet service providers), 6
    compared to AOL, 113

J-K

keyboard shortcuts, 20-22, 69, 86
Keyword keyword, 34
keywords, 19-20, 34-35
    AOL Insider, 159
    AOL Live, 34
    AOL Store, 46
    Ask-A-Teacher, 66
    Billing, 113, 152

Buddy, 83
BuddyView, 85
Channels, 28
Connectix, 126
Entertainment, 53
Games, 55
Gopher, 111
Grandstand, 58
Help, 149
Homework Help, 66
Influence, 63
Instant Messenger, 82
Internet, 106, 127
Keyword, 34
Mail Controls, 161
Mailing Lists, 112
Members, 86
MHM, 151
Movies, 54
My Home Page, 116
Neighborhood Watch, 164
NetFind, 111
Netscape, 125
News, 60
News Profiles, 62
Newsgroups, 109
Newsstand, 63
Notify AOL, 141, 160, 168-169
  security, 80
Parental Controls, 165-166
PC Graphics, 120
PC Help, 33
Personal Publisher, 116
Premium, 57
Preview, 162
PrimeHost, 123
Research & Learn, 64
Slideshows, 62
Sports, 57
System Response, 160
TOS, 76, 168
Virus, 141
WWW, 108

L-M

links to World Wide Web,
  channels, 26

local connections, 8
  finding additional access
    numbers, 14-17
Log Manager, message board
  postings, 98
log-on, 12-13
LOL (Laughing Out Loud)
  smiley, 105

MacInTax tax forums, 42
magazines, Newsstand, 63
Mail Center drop-down menu, 25
maintenance shutdowns, 159
marketing information, Internet commerce, PrimeHost, 37-39
  see also business information
master account name, 34
Member Directory, 34, 86-87
Member Help Interactive chat room,
  152-154
Member Services, help, 149-150
Members Helping Members forum,
  151-152
Members' Choice keyword, 34
merchandise, ordering, 46-48
  guidelines, 49-50
message boards
  compared to email, 88-89
  first-time visits, 93-95
  ground rules, 95
  messages disappearing, 160
  organization, 89-90
  posting messages, 90-92, 96
    online etiquette, 97
    responses, 98
  preferences, 92
  visiting, Automatic AOL
    sessions, 136
Microsoft Internet Explorer
  limitations, 126-127
  speeding performance with
    Connectix Surf Express, 126
mIRC (Khaled Mardam-Bey)
  installing/configuring, 128
  using, 129-130
modems, 2
  checking types, 6-8
  problems, 156-158

movies forums, 54-55
Movies keyword, 54
My AOL drop-down menu, 18-19,
    25
My Files drop-down menu, 25

N

Names keyword, 34
navigating AOL
    keywords, 19-20
    message boards, 94-95
    toolbar icons, 22-25
Neighborhood Watch, 164
    Parental Controls, 165-167
NetFind, 111
NetMail, 127
Netscape Navigator, 125
    limitations, 126-127
    speeding performance with
        Connectix Surf Express, 126
news behind the news (Influence
    channel), 64
News Channel, 60-62
News Profiles, 62
newsgroups, 109-110
    custom settings for
        children, 167
newspapers, Newsstand, 63

O

Offline Reading feature, 19
OIC (Oh, I See) smiley, 105
online conferences, 34
online etiquette
    chat rooms, 100-104
    message boards, 97
online Rolodex, see Address Book
Open Image dialog box, 71
ordering merchandise, 46-50

P

Parental Controls, 19, 165-166
    customizing, 166-167
    keyword, 35
passwords, 11
    Automatic AOL sessions,
        136-137

PC Help desk forum structure, 33
People Connection Town Square,
    99-101
People drop-down menu, 25
Personal Filing Cabinet
    saving email, 76
    storing email for Automatic
        AOL sessions, 139
Personal Finance channel, 39, 41
Personal Publisher, 115-117
    Web pages
        background art, 118-119
        clip art, 119-120
        previewing, 121-122
        templates, 117-118
        text, 120-121
        titles/headlines, 118
        viewing, 122
photos, see graphics
Picture Gallery feature, 71
pictures, see graphics
posting messages on message boards,
    96
    online etiquette, 97
    reading, 90-922
    responses, 98
preferences, message boards, 92
Preferences Guide feature, 19
Premium Games, 57
Premium keyword, 57
PrimeHost, 37-39
problems
    accessing FTP sites, 162
    AOL
        accessing from
            Macintoshes, 156
        customizing toolbar,
            155-156
        installing latest
            version, 155
        requests for passwords or
            credit card information,
            160
        shutdown for
            maintenance, 159
        slow responses to requests,
            159-160

sound, 159
system crashes during
  AOL connections, 162
message boards, messages
  disappearing, 160
modems, 156-158
unsolicited email, 160-161
Web sites, slow access or
  inaccessible, 161
programs
  Connectix Surf Express, 126
  IRC client, 127-128
  mIRC, 128-130
  NetMail, 127
  see also software
public domain software, 148

Q-R

QuickStart keyword, 35
Quotes & Portfolios center, 41-42
quoting portions of messages in
  replies, 74-75

replying to email, 74-75
Research & Learn channel, 64-66
responding to messages on message
  boards, 98
Rolodex (online), *see* Address Book
rules, message boards, 95

S

saving email, 76
screen names, 10-11
  for other family members, 164
  passwords, 11
security
  anti-virus software, 140-141
  downloading files, 76
  Notify AOL, 80
  passwords, 11
sending email
  AOL, 70-71
  Instant Messages, 79-85
  Internet, 71-72
  with attached files, 75-76
servers, IRC, AOL, 130-132
services, Find Central, 28-32

setup, AOL, 6-8
  account information, 9-10
  local connections, 8
  master account name, 34
  My AOL screen, 18-19
  passwords, 11
  screen names, 10-11
shareware, 147
  mIRC (Khaled Mardam-Bey),
    128-130
Shopping channel, 45
  ordering merchandise, 46-50
shutdowns for maintenance, 159
smileys, 104-105
software
  anti-virus, 140-141
  commercial, 147
  demoware, 147
  freeware, 148
  latest available, 148
  public domain, 148
  shareware, 147
  see also programs
software libraries
  channels, 26
  finding/downloading files,
    140, 147
    available types, 147-148
    Download Help Center,
      150-151
    Download Later option,
      144-146
    Download Now option,
      143-144
    File Search, 141-143
    resuming downloads, 146
    using downloaded
      files, 146
sound problems, 159
Sports channel, 57-59
Start menu, Windows 95, adding
  AOL, 5-6
stocks, checking, 41-42
styles for type, formatting email,
  69-70
system crashes during AOL
  connections, 162

T

Tax forums, 42-44
Tax Planning features, 42-44
Tech Live, *see* Member Help
   Interactive chat room
templates
      Personal Publisher Web pages,
      117-118
            background art, 118-119
            clip art, 119-120
            text, 120-121
            titles/headlines, 118
      PrimeHost Web sites, 39
Terms of Service (TOS), 12
      downloading files, 76
      guidelines for children
      online, 168
text, Web pages, 120-121
text alignment, formatting email,
   69-70
titles, Web pages, 118
Toolbar icons
      adding personal ones, 24
      commands, 22-25
      navigating AOL, 22-25
      program features, 22-25
toolbars, customizing, problems,
   155-156
Top News Story, 60
Top Tips keyword, 35
transferring files
      across Internet, 110
      from unknown sources,
      140-141
      see also downloading files
Travel channel, 50-52
TTFN (Ta-Ta For Now) smiley, 105
TTYL (Talk To You Later)
   smiley, 105
TurboTax tax forums, 42

U-V

Upgrade keyword, 35
uploading files, 140, 148
Usenet, 109-110

Virus Information Center, 141
viruses, protecting against, 140-141

W-Z

weather, Your Weather, 60
Web browsers, 108
      Internet Explorer
      (Microsoft), 124
            limitations, 126-127
            speeding performance
            with Connectix Surf
            Express, 126
      Navigator (Netscape)
            limitations, 126-127
            speeding performance
            with Connectix Surf
            Express, 126
Web hosting services, 123
Web pages, 115-116
      for businesses, 123
      Personal Publisher, 116-117
            background art, 118-119
            clip art, 119-120
            previewing, 121-122
            templates, 117-118
            text, 120-121
            titles/headlines, 118
            viewing, 122
Web sites
      inaccessible, 161
      PrimeHost, 39
      slow access, 161
      see also Internet
Welcome window, 12-13
Windows 3.*x*, installing AOL, 2, 4
Windows 95
      adding AOL to Start menu, 5-6
      installing AOL, 2-4
Windows 98, installing AOL, 3-4
WorkPlace Channel, 36-37
World Wide Web links, channels, 26
      see also Internet, Web sites
writing email, 68-69

Your Weather, 60